THE COMPLETE PREGNANCY GUIDE FOR MEN

THE ULTIMATE HANDBOOK FOR FIRST-TIME DADS AND EXPECTING FATHERS NAVIGATING PREGNANCY AND POST-BIRTH WITH CONFIDENCE

ALEX CIRILLO

CONTENTS

INTRODUCTION

The nature of impending fatherhood is that you are doing something that you are unqualified to do, and then you become qualified while doing it.

— JOHN GREEN

It happened! My wife and I were fast asleep when that newborn boy of mine started whining. Now, either my wife had a long day and was knocked out, or she was pretending not to hear our little bundle of joy screaming to the top of his lungs, demanding a diaper change. I thought for a moment about pretending to be asleep and making my wife get up to change him, but I just couldn't lay there while my son lay in a wet diaper. After all, I wouldn't want to be sitting in soggy britches, either.

Manning up, I decided, "I got this," climbed out of bed, and headed for my boy's bedroom. It was a typical middle-of-the-night diaper change, and I felt pretty good about myself. There was definitely nothing to be scared of. I had successfully changed a few diapers before and thought I had this whole dad thing down pat. But little did I know, this diaper change would be one for the books.

I scooped up my little twin from his crib and laid him down on the changing table, talking to him in the funny voice we tend to use when talking to kids. I carefully began removing the dirty diaper as I said to him, "Who's a stinky lil' boy? You're the stinky one, that's for sure." I was about to tell him just how bad his butt actually stunk when suddenly, I heard a little noise. I told myself, *Don't worry, it is just a little fart, which is no big deal. He gets it from his daddy.* But, dang, this boy stunk!

Boy, let me tell you, I was wrong–I'll admit it. I would soon see that this wasn't one of those farts for which a dad is proud of his child. Nope, this wasn't one of those at all. Suddenly, another little squirt sound must have felt good because the little turd giggled. I thought he was laughing because of the sound, but I was wrong about that too. This little son of a gun was laughing at what was about to take place because he would be the cause of the war that was only seconds from taking place. After the giggle was another little sound that came from his booty, but this sound was not coming alone this time.

The little poot was quickly followed by greenish-yellow runny turds, shooting straight out the boy's butt, not caring where they landed. They were flying everywhere. In a matter of seconds, I was being hit with projectile poop missiles coming out from every single direction. I didn't even have time to dunk or dodge the stinky mess. It was very much like playing a game of dodgeball, except with poop instead of clean dodgeballs! I guess you all know who won the game. It sure as hell wasn't me.

My son hit me all over with poop squirts. The stinky mess landed in my hair and shirt, smacked me in my face, and just got everywhere! To make matters worse, my wife must have woken up from her fake sleeping after I decided to be a good husband and change the kid because I suddenly heard more giggling–and it wasn't the baby's giggles! I turned around with poop dripping from my chin, and there she was, standing, bent over, grabbing her stomach, and laughing so hard that tears were rolling down her cheeks. I couldn't believe it, but I began to laugh too. I'm sure I would have been a sight to see with my new poop hair gel, freckles, and fashion line.

I knew right then and there, at that moment, that being a dad is full of fun and unpleasant surprises. I learned that when you are a father, you must expect the unexpected, even during regular diaper changes. However, this is when my wife realized that she would be handling the majority of diaper changes from then on.

RELAX, HELP IS HERE

If you're reading this book, then you are probably very nervous. Sure, when you first discovered that you were about to have a mini-you, you couldn't wait to tell all the boys. However, I also know that the wave of anxiety and fear of becoming a father has probably kicked in full force in less than a week tops.

Believe me; I get it. You're worried about what changes your significant other will undergo while pregnant. You would like to know just as much as your partner does about how your little baby-to-be is developing. Intimacy has probably crossed your mind more than a few times too. You are probably wondering if it is okay to have sex at all or if it will hurt your baby. I'm sure that fear of being a father has set in, too. Some of you may be worried about whether you even have the money in the bank for a baby right now.

Just take a deep breath and relax because help is here. My name is Alex Cirillo. I am the father of three wonderful kids, one boy, and two girls. I'm a family coach and often do speaking events to help families through their struggles and hard times. I've also helped some overcome the fear of fatherhood. Now, I am here to help you quiet that little voice in your head telling you that you should fear fatherhood and help you learn to embrace and welcome it instead. What better time to start being a great dad than the minute you know you will be a father?

Not every child is blessed with a good father. Most people don't take the time to stop and think about how not having a father could affect a child. Both girls and boys need their fathers in their lives. However, I know the pain of this all too well.

I didn't have the perfect childhood when I was a little boy. Instead of a loving, fun father that some little boys are blessed to have, I had a cold, distant father who would eventually leave while I was still young. Man, the hurt I felt watching other children rough house and play with their dads hurt me deeply. There were times I needed a father's advice and help but had no one. Until you *don't* have a father, you won't ever really understand how painful it is for a child not to have one.

The pain can be felt forever, which is why I don't understand how the same children like me, who had no father around growing up, could put their children through the same thing. Most men who have absent fathers grow up only to repeat the cycle. They make their children feel the same pain their father put them through growing up. If you felt the pain of not having a father, then you know the exact pain that you are causing your child when you walk out on them. I am not like those guys nor do I understand their way of thinking.

The fact that you are taking the time to learn more about pregnancy and fatherhood shows that you are not like those guys, either. I can't just walk away from my family because I remember how I felt when my dad walked out. I promised myself that day that, when I grew up, I would be the father I wished I had for my children. Honestly, I did not repeat the cycle and kept the promise I made to myself. Now, my life mission is to help families navigate through all the fun ups and the low downs of parenting and empower parents to raise healthy and happy little children.

Some of you may have even purchased this book because you didn't have a loving father either, and you

1

FROM SPECTATOR TO TEAMMATE

The way the team plays as a whole determines its success.

— BABE RUTH

"**I** love being a dad. Fatherhood is the best thing that could happen to me," Kobe Bryant, a loving father, and husband, once said.

We all know Kobe Bryant, right? He was one of the best basketball players that ever walked this planet. Basketball is what he is known for. Bryant spent his whole 20-year career playing in the NBA for the Los Angeles Lakers. Although he was a beast on the court, there was something else, besides basketball, that he did besides shooting hoops–and that was being a father. Kobe and his wife, Vanessa, had four beautiful girls together: Gianna Maria-Onore, Natalia Diamante, Bianka Bella, and Capri Kobe.

On the rainy morning of January 26, 2020, the unexpected happened. Kobe and his daughter, Gianna Maria-Onore, woke up and headed to his private helicopter to fly to a basketball game. The weather that day was not the best by any means. The sky was full of dark clouds, and it had been raining off and on. While in the air, the pilot had difficulties that he did not have time to react to, causing the helicopter to go spiraling down, crashing into the side of a mountain in Calabasas at 9:45 am.

The NBA Superstar and his sweet, beautiful daughter Gianna didn't survive the horrific crash. God called them both home together. Kobe, Gianna, and seven other passengers who were on the helicopter lost their lives in the horrific crash.

Kobe Bryant was remembered for his success in the NBA and for being an outstanding father. You would think that he would have wished for a boy to follow his athletic legacy. However, Kobe Bryant didn't need a boy to follow in his footsteps. His girls followed in his footsteps, and he didn't, and wouldn't, want it any other way.

Kobe was proud of being a "girl dad," as he called it. He thought that fatherhood was the best thing that happened to him. There weren't many times that you would see him without one of his daughters. They were his pride and joy, and he was a perfect father to each one.

Just like you thought, Kobe probably was a little nervous before his first child made her grand entrance. He may have worried even more because of his fame. However, as we can see, his worry quickly vanished once his pretty little bundle of joy arrived in this world. The same will be true for you as well. Once your child is here, you too will know that you got this and everything will work out.

THE CHANGING AMERICAN FAMILY

Kobe Bryant was such a great father because he still believed in traditional family morals, values, and respect. It's no secret that everyday family life in America has been changing and changing rather quickly, especially the role that fathers play. In the past, although my father left, most children had their father in their household. More parents are divorced now, unlike when marriage was a lifelong commitment. Fathers, when I was growing up, were the family's breadwinners. Mothers usually stayed home, kept the house up, raised the children, and had dinner waiting on the table when the father came home from work.

We have seen a total shift in this usual way of living lately. It seems as if fathers leaving the family is the norm now. Single women struggle to make ends meet by themselves and raise their children on their own. What is shocking to me is how we allow so many men to neglect their children without punishment. If a woman were to neglect her child, she would be taken to jail for child neglect. Today, however, men neglect their children like it's nothing and have nothing to worry about if they choose to do so.

Women have become the money makers of the family, and most don't get to come home to dinner on the table like men did when I was growing up. This scenario may seem like no big deal right now, but in a few moments, you will see how this negatively impacts growing children. Studies have shown that a child's bond with their father is just as important as a child's bond with his mother (Brott, 2022).

HOW CHILDREN BENEFIT FROM HAVING ENGAGED FATHERS

Many people believe that a child is fine as long as the child's mother is in their life, but that is furthest from the truth. Children want and need their fathers. There are many ways a child benefits from having an actively involved father.

Children with involved fathers score higher on cognitive milestone tests and motor development tests. Those with actively involved fathers have superior problem-solving and adaptive skills (Brott, 2022).

A child with an engaged father tends to be more sociable and creative (Brott, 2022). They are so much more outgoing because their fathers tend to be. Fathers give children the confidence to try doing more things themselves. Mothers are usually busier and don't like messes, so they do more things for their children instead of encouraging them to try more things themselves. On the other hand, fathers are messy, so they don't mind the mess. They are playful and talk to more people. When a child is trying to do something, they wait and see if the child can figure it out before they intervene. When fathers step in to help their children, they usually teach them how to do it instead of just doing it for them.

The effect fathers have on a child's language is phenomenal. Fathers tend to speak to their children in ways that stretch the child's vocabulary. They also ask children more "wh-" questions–who, what, when, where, and why–and make more requests for clarification from the child. This encourages conversation and builds vocabulary (Brott, 2022).

When a father is not involved in a child's life, the child feels unwanted. They don't understand why other children have their fathers and they don't. One child I know feels like his father traded him in. His father left their family for a woman whose son played on his basketball team. His father stopped seeing him, making him feel like he wasn't good enough.

Young women who don't have involved fathers tend to go through depression a lot more than those who do. She will also never really understand how a man should love her and thus allows men to treat her in any kind of way. The young woman will go to extremes for a man she is dating, usually out of fear of him leaving like her father did.

Many children without engaged fathers are abused physically and sexually by their mother's boyfriends (ASPE, 2005); not all children in this situation experience this, but a good many. They have to deal with new men entering and out of their lives. The boyfriends of some mothers will move into their house and disrupt their normality. Children will have different sets of rules every time a new man comes along.

Children need structure, so you must be involved in your child's life, even if you are not with their mother. In the same way, the mother can take you to court; you can do the same for visitation rights. Some women can be complicated to get along with and even try to keep you from your child. Some will be spiteful and put you on child support even when you are taking care of your child.

Fathers do have rights, though. However, for a father to get his rights, he has to take some steps before they are granted to him. Each state is different, but the first step in every state is establishing paternity. Before a man can assert any rights in regard to the care of a child he had out of marriage, he must first prove his paternity for the child. Hopefully, this is not your situation and never will be, but if so, then know this is the first step in getting your rights.

The role of a father in shaping a child's life is undeniable. From providing emotional support to setting an example and being a positive role model, fathers play a crucial role in the development and well-being of their children. Both you and your children will benefit greatly from your involvement in their lives. After all, you owe it to them.

My father was the type of man who wasn't comfortable with physical affection. He was a stern, distant man who rarely showed any emotion, let alone the love I needed. As a result, I grew up feeling emotionally detached and struggled to express my feelings or accept physical affection from others.

The relationship I had with my father was strained, and I always felt like something was missing. I longed for the warmth and love that I saw other children receiving from their fathers because I never received it from my own. As I grew up, I found that the lack of emotion and expression I got from my father affected my relationships with others.

I also struggled to connect with partners and tended to push them away. As a result, this left me feeling lonely, despite being surrounded by friends and family. When I reached my late 20s, I realized my father's behavior's impact on my own. I decided to seek therapy to work through my feelings. Now I help others do the same because it's never too late to change and become involved. Throughout the book, you may see things repeated, but that is because they are essential, and some things in pregnancy last more than one trimester.

2

THE PREGAME WARM-UP

It's not pressure unless you are not prepared.

— COLIN KAEPERNICK

P regnancy is like preparing for a big game. You and your child's mother are now teammates whether you want to be or not. Just as teams need the right equipment, training, and winning strategy, so do the two of you. You should ensure that both of you are mentally and physically prepared for anything pregnancy throws at you. If not, you may get blindsided along the way by many different things–and you would hate for that to happen on game day when your baby arrives.

A friend of mine was blindsided a few times during game time when her child made his grand entrance. She got pretty big during her pregnancy, so everyone thought her baby would be huge. All they bought was a few newborn outfits, but most were in bigger sizes.

When it was finally time, and Junior made his entrance into this world, they were shocked to see that he wasn't that big at all. The baby was only six pounds and skinny —none of the clothes they brought to the hospital fit. Safe to say, his wife started to freak out.

She worried he would get cold. Not to mention, the baby still had to take newborn pictures, and she didn't want him to be naked in the photos. All the clothes she tried on him swallowed him whole. Junior's dad tried to save the day. He got in his car and headed to Walmart. Once in Walmart, he headed for the baby clothes, thinking this would be a piece of cake. However, when he got to the baby clothes, they had absolutely no preemie clothes. Just when he was about to give up, he noticed some preemie outfits hiding on the back of a rack. He quickly grabbed one and died laughing when he saw it.

Oh well, he thought to himself as he drove quickly back to the hospital. His thinking was at least it was something for his child to wear. He pulled into the hospital parking lot, ran to the elevator, and went straight to his girlfriend's hospital room. When he opened the door, she got all excited, thinking he would have many outfits for her to play dress up with on her new baby boy. However, my friend cried when he pulled the outfit out of the bag.

"A Christmas tuxedo? That was the best you could do? Couldn't you get more than one outfit? Do you really think I wanted my baby's first photos in a Christmas tuxedo? He was born in September. September!" she hissed at him. It was the funniest thing I ever saw now that it is in the past, but at the time, it was no laughing matter. At least, not to her anyways. However, the child's father and I laughed about it in the hospital hall, where she could not hear. The point is you want to avoid being in his position. It is better to get a game plan ready right now.

You may have no clue where to start. That's okay because I am going to help you out. There are things you can do as a father to encourage your child's mother, doing your part to make sure everything goes smoothly during the pregnancy. Below you will find some topics that are really important to know about during pregnancy:

SEXUAL INTERCOURSE DURING PREGNANCY

Sexual intercourse may not be as important as other things, but I'm sure it has crossed your mind a few times. Having sexual intercourse is perfectly fine during pregnancy. In fact, once your child's mother gets close to her due date, doctors will actually encourage you to have sexual intercourse. Sexual intercourse around the due date will help break your significant other's water, which is great. You don't have to worry about hurting the baby during sexual intercourse, either. The Fetus is in the mother's uterus, not in her vagina. No, you will not poke the child during intercourse. Pay attention to your partner and how they feel about sexual intercourse as well. If she is not comfortable in one position, try a different one. And, don't forget, when it gets close to the baby's due date, have more sexual intercourse than usual to aid in getting that baby out of that belly. If your partner has a high-risk pregnancy, always consult the doctor first.

SMOKING, DRUGS, AND ALCOHOL

I am sure you all know that smoking during pregnancy can cause your child some problems. If your child's mother continues to smoke during pregnancy, there are risks to the child's health, such as damage to the child's tissue, brain, and lungs. Studies have also shown that smoking during pregnancy is linked to cleft lips in newborns. There is also a chance of premature birth and other complications (Lie et al., 2008). I will say that if your child's mother does smoke, you should understand that she may need help to stop. I also know a few people who smoked during their pregnancy, and nothing was wrong with their babies. That being said, every pregnancy is different, so you should play it safe than sorry and help her quit smoking if she does.

Alcohol and drugs are other stories. Drinking or doing drugs is a massive no-no in pregnancy. When babies are born addicted to drugs or alcohol, the withdrawals alone could kill them. They develop physical and mental problems that will never go away. More importantly, using drugs and alcohol during pregnancy is associated with high miscarriage rates (UCSF Health, 2022). You have the right to decide to do drugs and alcohol, but you do not have the right to choose to get your baby hooked on them. Just say no during pregnancy.

PRENATAL VITAMINS

Do you know how many athletes use steroids to increase their performance? Well, prenatal vitamins are kind of like steroids for pregnant women. They make sure that the mother and baby perform at their best. Babies suck a lot of nutrients from their mothers. Sometimes the mother may have vitamin deficiencies, which is dangerous for the mother since the few vitamins she consumes are consumed by the baby first and foremost. Many women become anemic during pregnancy and need additional iron supplements, mainly to prevent blood transfusions at birth. Babies also take a lot of calcium from mothers during pregnancy, which results in the mother getting cavities and poor dental health. Prenatal vitamins are essential, so it is up to you to encourage your partner to see doctors–and that includes the dentist!

EVALUATE YOUR JOB

If you are unemployed, now is an excellent time to start looking for a job. You will need a way to take care of your child. Not only will you need to take care of your child's necessities, but it also makes you feel better when you can. Knowing that you can get medicine and diapers if your child needs them takes a lot of stress off of yourself and your relationship.

LIVING SITUATION

Children need room to grow. Around this time, you should evaluate whether your house or apartment is large enough to accommodate your growing family. In today's day and time, especially if this would be your first child, knowing if your home is suitable and within your budget can be difficult. When a baby comes into the picture, though, it's a must. A child needs their own room and space. However, if you are living with others (maybe hoping to save up some money for your own place), this is the time to start looking for a new home. When you live with other people, they tend not to respect your boundaries, even if they are your parents. Having your place is very beneficial for you, your child, and your relationship with your significant other.

LEARN YOUR FAMILY HISTORY

Doctors will want to know what diseases run in both your and your partner's families. It's good to know these things ahead of time before any complications show up so that the doctor is on the lookout and prepared if they do arise.

MAINTAIN A HEALTHY WEIGHT

You should encourage your partner to maintain a healthy weight during pregnancy, and you should keep a healthy weight too. Pregnancy can be very uncomfortable, and the more weight you put on, the worse it is. Women can also get diabetes during pregnancy, so they must be cautious of this. You, too, will need to maintain your weight because your baby will keep you running around and want to play a lot. It is easier to care for a child when you are healthy and have energy.

CHEMICALS

Your partner should not be around certain things during pregnancy. Certain chemicals can be very harmful to your unborn baby. Even hair dye chemicals can have adverse effects on a fetus. It is best to always read chemical labels. One important thing that pregnant women cannot handle is cat litter. If you have a cat, the litter box is now your job, buddy.

STRESS

Your partner is dealing with a lot right now. We know you are too, but your partner's body is creating a whole new person inside her. Hormones and emotions are

running wild inside of her. She is worried about gaining weight and her body changing shape. She is concerned about labor and delivery. Not to mention, in the back of her mind, she is probably also worried that she will not be a good mother. Try to understand that she is stressed and anxious. Try not to add to this with uncalled-for bickering and fighting. Arguing during pregnancy is not healthy for your partner or your baby-to-be.

THE TEAM HUDDLE

A lot of changes are about to happen in your life when your baby gets here. So it is crucial that you and your partner take time to discuss and ask each other some important questions. The two of you are on the same team, so you need to be on the same page in the play-book. Being open and honest with each other can help you easily navigate struggles and challenges when they arise because you already have a plan. Below are some questions to get the conversation started so the two of you will be ready for whatever surprises life throws at you:

1. What morals, values, and principles did your parents raise you with that are important to you to raise your child to follow?

2. When you were a child, was there anything your parents, or any other adult, did around you that you did not want to be done around your child, and why?

3. When you got in trouble as a child, whether you deserved it or not, how were you punished by your parents or other adults? What are your thoughts about how you were disciplined? Could you have been disciplined more, less, not as harshly, or in another more effective way?

4. In what ways do you plan on disciplining your child so that they know right from wrong and grow up to be respectful young men or women?

5. What are some of the many ways you will make time for your relationship with your partner?

6. How do you both plan to make sure you both get time to yourself after the arrival of your little MVP? Personal time is very important because every member of the team needs a breather sometimes.

7. Will the two of you teach your child a religion, and if so, which one?

8. What is the name of the team the baby will play on? In other words, whose last name with the little one be so blessed to carry on?

9. You must set boundaries for your parents, friends, and family. They need to know where

the line is and the consequences of crossing them. What boundaries do you not want others to cross when it comes to your parenting and child?

10. Have you considered childcare for when one of you can't be there? What happens when you both decide to keep working?

11. Will the mother decide to breastfeed or bottle-feed her growing baby? If you plan to bottle feed, have you thought about what brand and kind of formula you will use?

12. Will the little one be sleeping in a bassinet, crib, or with the two of you? Do you know the pros and cons of the baby sleeping alone and co-sleeping with the child?

13. Is momma going to have a planned c-section or vaginal birth? If vaginal birth, does momma know all her options? Has she ever thought about home water births? Does she plan on having the baby with an epidural, or will she do this all-natural with no meds?

14. Who would you like to be with the two of you in the delivery room?

15. Circumcision is highly recommended by me as a man, also by doctors, and by some religions. Do you plan on having your baby circumcised if you are expecting a boy?

16. Will you have a gender reveal party to find out the sex of the child, or do you want to know as soon as the doctor does?
17. What do you plan to do if you find out that the Fetus has genetic differences?
18. Is the pregnancy normal or high-risk?
19. How does momma plan on getting sleep? How can you help her to get some rest after the baby arrives?
20. Have you chosen a pediatrician for the baby yet? The choice of a pediatrician needs to be made before the momma gives birth.

Many men get overwhelmed with all that comes with pregnancy. One of their main worries is whether or not they will be able to afford this whole pregnancy and baby. Sometimes it gets to be too much for them. There were not many books for men to teach them about the pregnancy until this one, to show men that things would be okay. Yes, sure, pregnancy does cost a lot. The Peterson-Kaiser Family Foundation Health Symptom Tracker (2022) has estimated the total cost of pregnancy, childbirth, and postpartum care to be roughly $18,865. They believe that the patient must pay nearly $3,000 of that total amount out of pocket.

Yes, that is a rather large amount of money. Do not worry, though, because if you cannot afford it due to low income like most Americans, you have options. Mothers who have low incomes qualify for many programs that offer assistance to low-income mothers and families. These programs will cover all the costs of doctor visits for both the mother and child and food for the mother and child.

There are three main programs, some depending on the family's income that every family should know about and apply for during pregnancy, and four programs after the child arrives. We will discuss the programs for after the child is born a little later. Before giving birth, women can first apply for the following:

1. **Medicaid:** Insurance is vital for you during and after your pregnancy, for yourself and the baby after it's born. Medicaid will cover all the costs of your doctor's visits during pregnancy and for the babies after pregnancy. You can also stay on Medicaid after giving birth to ensure you stay healthy as well. Medicaid covers all the baby's costs, and there are no out-of-pocket fees. Medicaid also covers the cost of medications. Children's prescriptions are free of charge with Medicaid. As you can see, Medicaid is ideal for low-income families, so keep it in mind.
2. **WIC:** Wic is a must for all moms. WIC gives you vouchers for fresh and healthy foods. Not

only is it a lifesaver for food during pregnancy, but also for formula after the baby arrives.

3. **Food Stamps:** Food Stamps are a savior for many families nationwide. The program gives low-income families a debit card with monthly deposits for anything in the grocery store besides hot or fast food. Many families get over $400 monthly food stamps to feed their families. You can apply for food stamps before or after the baby is born.

These programs have been a lifesaver for many expecting families. They cover the cost of doctors, prescriptions, and food. However, there are also many other things a newborn baby will need. So let's make a list of some of the things that are important for you to have when your baby arrives and discuss the cost of them for a moment:

- **Carseat:** These things are essential to have. Take it from me; you want to travel with a car seat. When one car slams into another, the impact is powerful. The force of impact is much stronger than your baby's weight. It is best to get a car seat that grows with your baby. You can even find car seat travel systems, including a car seat and stroller. Car seat travel systems are the best option.

- ○ Price: Starts at $100
- ○ Cost of travel system: $214

- **Crib:** A crib is only needed if you plan on letting the baby sleep in the crib. Most of the time, people buy a crib, but the child ends up sleeping with their momma or in a bassinet.

  - ○ Price: Starts at $150

- **Crib Mattress:** If you decide to go with the crib, you should know that most cribs do not include mattresses.

  - ○ Price: Starts at $40

- **Glider or Rocking Chair:** This is a must-have. I would buy this before anything on this list. Putting a baby to sleep with no rocker can be pretty difficult. I highly recommend buying one of these.

  - ○ Price: Starts at $179

- **Baby Swing:** This is another must that babies love.

  ○ Price: Starts at $73

- **Bassinet:** These are great to have if you want to avoid using a crib and last a long time.

  ○ Price: Starts at $70

- **Changing Table:** You will see why these are a must-have when the baby makes a big nasty squirt.

  ○ Price: Starts at $100

- **Bottles:** DO NOT BUY CHEAP BOTTLES! A cheap bottle will trap air bubbles in the baby's belly, resulting in screaming cries from a belly full of gas.

  ○ Price of good bottles: $22 a pack

- **Breast Pump:** Don't go cheap here, either. A woman's breast should be cared for while breastfeeding. Breastfeeding can be painful. A good pump makes things a lot easier.

  o Price: Starts at $28

- **Diaper Bag:** A must-have for on-the-go parents. It helps keep everything the baby needs in one place.

  o Price: Starts at $20

The things on the following list are the little things you should buy. Most of them can be bought for under $10. Therefore, I will not include the prices of these items, but they are just as important to purchase as the items above.

- Burp clothes
- Clothing
- Washcloths
- Nursery decor
- Baby Toys
- Teethers
- Towels
- Baby healthcare/grooming set

- Mittens (You really, really need these so the baby doesn't scratch their face up)
- Tylenol or Motrin
- Gas drops
- Stock up on baby food

This all probably sounds a little overwhelming, right? The cost seems too much and may even scare you, but don't let it. Most of these things you will get from your family and friends at the baby shower. Many baby stores online will allow you to set up a baby registry. When you do, the guest you invite for your baby shower can go online and purchase things from your baby registry from whatever site you choose to register at. Including where you are registered on the baby shower invitation is a good idea.

Also, on your baby shower invitation, you should ask that people buy diapers bigger than newborn sizes. It is better that you buy a couple of packs of newborn diapers and let your guests buy bigger sizes because babies grow super fast. They will only be in newborn diapers for a few weeks at most.

All doctor's expenses will be covered if you are eligible for Medicaid. Each trimester, you will undergo essential steps and tests to ensure that momma and the baby are in good health. Medicaid covers the cost of all these things. We will discuss each of the tests in the corresponding chapters.

When my wife and I found out we were about to add a new addition to our family for the first time, I got excited—after the shock had settled down. I spent months going to birthing classes, remodeling the spare room to be a baby-proof nursery, and making sure my child's mother got everything she was craving to eat.

After the big day and we brought our first child home, it didn't take long to see that this baby was costing us a big chunk of change. We decided to see just how much our baby cost a month, and when we saw the total of the things we had bought just for the baby that month, I didn't think we would ever have enough money for anything but the baby.

I was really worried about how we would make it financially. Over the next few months, I began to realize that, even though the baby was costing us a good bit of money, we never really missed the income more than we did *before* we had our first child. I would give everything I own for my child, so it was well worth it. There will always be challenges along the way. Know that your family will make it with the love and support of your extended family and close friends.

I wish I had known the cost of a baby beforehand and that my father would have taught me about fatherhood. I needed to learn many things about becoming a dad that I just had to learn on my own. That's why I decided to assist new parents and parents-to-be so they can know about pregnancy and its cost. Sure, you will be okay, even if no one does. But if someone guides you, you will be better mentally, emotionally, and financially prepared.

Not only should pregnant women and their partners be prepared for a baby, but those expecting to adopt should be too. My friend's brother can't have kids. His little swimmers don't swim fast enough, making him a sterile man. His sister knew a woman who always had babies and gave them up for adoption. She knew this woman was pregnant.

My friend put the word in the lady's ear that her brother couldn't have children and was interested in adopting a child. She then introduced her friend and brother. On Christmas Eve, my friend's mother woke her up, telling her that her brother had a baby. She was lost for words.

The lady started to go into labor and called the brother —the important people here are the sister's friend, her brother, and his wife. The brother and his wife got to watch the baby be born and name her. They legally adopted the baby, and now that the child is older, when she feels upset, her daddy tells her, "I love you, baby girl. I wanted you so much. See?" He opened his top nightstand drawer and pulled out a piece of paper, "Daddy paid a lot of money for you. I will always love you."

This chapter covered the practical aspects, considerations, and questions to help you prepare for pregnancy. Now, in the next chapter, we will dive into the emotional side of things. Yes, that's right, it's time to talk about the rollercoaster of emotions that fatherhood can bring. From feeling overwhelmed and underprepared to battling negative beliefs and insecurities, it's natural for dads to experience a range of emotions during pregnancy. In the next chapter, we will explore the common emotional challenges fathers may face, dispel negative beliefs, and provide practical ways to be a supportive partner through it all.

3

BE A GREAT TEAMMATE

Every champion was once a contender that refused to give up.

— ROCKY BALBOA

Not long after my childhood friend, Chris, found out he would be a father, the other guys and I took him out to celebrate. We had a great day planned that we all needed. We were going to a college baseball game and then to the bar afterward for one last night of drinks and a good time before his baby touched down. Well, that was our plan anyway, but we never even made it to the ballfield. The bar didn't happen either.

While we were on the way to the game, we had to ride past a sewer plant. It was the kind of sewer plant that gets all the city's bathroom sewage. If you never rode past one of these, let me be the first to tell you that they were freaking stinking to high heavens; but it's nothing a man can't hold his breath and handle for a few seconds until you have driven past it.

We all began to smell the sewage before we even saw the plant. When we started smelling it, we all started joking about which of us let one rip. In the mix of us laughing and joking, Chris told us that he didn't feel so good. We all honestly thought he was poking fun like the rest of us and ignored him.

As we approached the sewage plant, he told us again that the smell of the plant was about to make him sick. We were all laughing and joking right before the smell hit us, so we thought he was playing around. Johnny, who was driving, thought it would be even funnier to speed up to give him a better whiff. Chris told Johnny right as we were finally passing the plant to pull over right then, or he was going to puke all over the back seat of his car.

Johnny finally figured that Chris might be serious this time. He asked him if he was playing or not. Chris tried to tell him that he was not playing, but before he could get the words out of his mouth, he threw up all over Greg, sitting in the backseat beside him. He also threw up all over Johnny's brand-new tan car seats and carpet.

Johnny finally got it through his thick skull that Chris actually was sick. He pulled the car over to the side of the road. When Johnny stopped the car, he got out and quickly opened the backdoor to check his car after being pushed out of the way by Chris so he could puke out the rest of his stomach contents.

Johnny was no longer a happy camper when he saw the disgusting mess Chris had made in the back of his car. But, in Chris's defense, he did try to warn him a few times. I didn't get a drop of throw-up on me, though, so I was okay. I found the situation hilarious.

Chris soon learned from his doctor that he had been having the same pregnancy symptoms as his child's mother. I know it sounds crazy, right? A man having pregnancy symptoms doesn't seem real, but it is. Chris had Couvade Syndrome. This syndrome, also known as "sympathetic pregnancy," is a condition where men experience pregnancy symptoms alongside their partners. Not only is this condition an actual physical phenomenon, but it's also a reminder to us that we men are just as involved in the pregnancy of our child as mothers are from the moment they find out that they are going to be a father.

Scary, right? Dang, right it is, but this is no time to be a baby–it's time to have a baby. So you have to get in the game and put your game face on. Make sure you pay close attention to your partner during this time. Don't do your partner how we did, Chris. If she feels sick in that car, you need to pull over, get out, and hold that lady's hair back for her.

So many different emotions and disagreements will arise between you and your partner now, which is normal. You are both probably scared. Your life is about to change drastically. Having emotions, both good and bad, are typical for you at this time.

You may think your life is over now, but it's not. Your life is just beginning. Once your child is here, you *won't* be able to picture life without them at all. You will love your child so much that you *don't* want to imagine a life without them. Having a child is one of the most rewarding things you can get out of life. A child is your creation with their mother. Only the two of you could have made that baby and no one else. That fact alone is amazing.

This is not the time to run off the field or forfeit the game. You may not be up to bat, but you're still in the game. If you care about your child, you should care about their mother, especially during pregnancy. Studies have shown that men involved during pregnancy reduce the mother's stress levels, making pregnancy safer for both her and the child (Coussons-Read, 2013).

BE YOUR TEAMMATE'S HYPE MAN

I love going to little league baseball games on Saturday afternoons. The young men are hilarious, competitive, and full of life. Young men are good at many different sports, but something about baseball gets them going. Not only are they good at playing ball, but they are also good at hyping each other up during the games. Children may see no big deal in hyping each other up and may even think of it as being silly and loud. They have no idea what hyping each other up does when they come up to bat, especially for their self-esteem. They don't realize the encouragement they are showing one another by being the batter's hype men.

When a batter from your team comes up to bat, the rest of the team doesn't walk around waiting for their turn to take a shot at getting a home run. Instead, the rest of the team presses their faces to the dugout fence or stands on the bench and stomps. Other players begin to clap when they spot the pitcher getting ready to sling the ball down to home plate. Then, all the players start chanting popular baseball chants, such as Home Run chants, if their player is up to bat.

The children stomp, clap, and cheer their way to victory by the end of the game. If the encouragement and motivation are good, then each ending of the game will be a success. However, if all the players on the team didn't pay attention, hype each other up, and cheer each other on, the game would be nowhere near as fun and much more stressful. Your team will only perform its best at any game nine times out of ten if the encouragement is on.

Pregnancy can be dangerous and come with many complications. Women's bodies also change very much during pregnancy. One thing many women struggle with the most during pregnancy is low self-esteem. Pregnancy does so much to a woman in nine little months. They gain weight and get scared that they will never lose it. They get stretch marks, and their bodies sometimes take on a new shape. Some women even start losing teeth due to the baby taking most of the calcium that the mother consumes.

When a woman goes through these changes, it's not easy for them emotionally. They worry that they will never get their shape back. Many also fear that their partner will leave them due to the changes that their bodies undergo. We even pick at them sometimes, not meaning any harm, about these things. Even though we may just be playing, and she may even laugh, they may have been hurt silently by your comments.

It's not comfortable being pregnant, I'm sure. Think about how we would feel if we had to carry another human's extra weight in our stomachs. Women have a lot of pressure on their hips and legs during pregnancy. The baby presses on all kinds of nerves, sending pain straight down their legs. The Fetus puts pressure on the spine as well. Breast pain in women, I've heard, is awful when the milk begins to fill in their breasts.

Inside your partner's body, a baby is growing. Yes, the man may have planted the seed, but a woman's body has to work to develop that seed and keep it alive. Your partner's body is doing its job of putting your child, its health, and safety first. A man's body will never have to care for two bodies instead of just one. We will never be able to understand everything our partner goes through now. That is why we have to make sure we are there the whole way to cheer them on.

If she is emotional sometimes, it's good to let her have her breakdown. Usually, it will only last a few minutes. When she gets it all out, give her a big hug, and refuse to let go until she feels better. You shouldn't walk away from the game unless you don't have a choice, meaning if she tells you to leave her alone or isn't in the mood to be touched. When labor time comes, cheer her on until that baby is out and crying. Tell her how good she looks if she is feeling ugly or big. Hype your partner up the same way the little league player hype their batters up when they step to the plate. Tell her you love her, she is glowing, and she is the most beautiful pregnant woman you have ever seen. Tell her that she is doing a great job when she gets overwhelmed. Let her know everything is okay and she has this under control. Most importantly, let her know that you are there for her if she needs anything at all.

WAYS TO BE A GOOD TEAMMATE DURING PREGNANCY

Sometimes it's hard to understand women and what they actually want us men to do when they are not pregnant. When they are pregnant, it only becomes more confusing. I spoke to a lady who has two children. I asked her to tell me how men could encourage them during pregnancy. She gave me some pretty good answers. Below are some of the common issues women have during pregnancy and how we can help them with these issues:

Weight Gain

Your significant other will gain weight; not might, but *will* gain weight! If they ask you if they are getting fat. Do not tell them yes! However, it would be best if you didn't lie to her either. Remind her that it is perfectly normal to gain weight because she has a baby growing inside her and that you like her body's changes. When she asks if she is getting fat, tell her she is not, but you love how well her booty or breasts look. Tell her that her body is just filling in all the parts of her body that you love. Women love it when their partner comments on how good their body looks. So take that as something you could highlight to make her feel better.

Cravings

Women crave a lot of crazy things when they are pregnant. The same lady who gave me some ideas about how we men could encourage and support their partner told me that, when she was pregnant, she made her children's father drive 45 minutes to Ryan's at 9:30 pm for bread. She wanted Ryan's rolls with their sweet butter and wasn't taking no for an answer. By him getting up to fetch her latest craving, despite the time, he made an excellent choice. Women cannot help what they are craving because it's not really them craving it but the baby in their stomach. Sometimes they will only stop craving a particular food once they get a taste of it.

It's better to get whatever crazy thing your partner wants to eat. After all, they feed us dinner every night— no need to fight over pickles and bread. You are now the "team mom" of your growing family, which now includes bringing snacks to the "game".

Pregnancy Pain

As mentioned earlier, pregnant women have many pregnancy pains. Some over-the-counter medications are dangerous to the baby. Two of these medications are ibuprofen and aspirin. These are the first things we would consider for pain, but you can't take these medications during pregnancy. They are dangerous for the Fetus that is growing. Instead, use Tylenol or speak to the doctor about the best pain medication to take.

You can do some things to help relieve her pain besides giving her medicine. Run your partner a nice warm bubble bath with Epsom salt when she is in pain. Put some candles around the tub, making her feel special and comfortable. Pregnant women's feet hurt a lot. Rub her feet if they are sore. Backrubs are great too. One type of massage you would like to give and that she would love is a butt massage. Don't laugh just yet. Your glutes are the largest muscle mass on your body, and you sit on them a lot. We never really realize how much we ignore this muscle group until we get a massage. Believe me; she will love it.

Morning Sickness

Morning sickness sucks for women. Some have it very bad, and some women don't get morning sickness at all. If your partner has morning sickness, make sure she eats a good meal at breakfast and dinner. Crackers in the morning have been known to help with morning sickness. Coca-Cola can aid in taking that queasy feeling away too, but make sure to keep consumption down to a can a day.

Always remember:

- Be understanding of your partner
- Listen, even if you disagree with her
- Be her advocate and look after her
- Attend whatever classes that she feels she needs
- Encourage naps
- Communicate with her
- Spend time together. A great book you could use for a date night with your partner is *Date Night Doozies*, by Marissa Partner. It is a great book with spicy, fun activities for you and your partner.
- Encourage her to take walks with you. The walks help when labor is soon to come.

IT TAKES TWO TO WIN THE GAME

When my wife was pregnant with our first child, she underwent many changes. She was also highly emotional. It seemed like she was always moody and tired. She would even snap at me for saying good morning sometimes. I didn't understand everything she was going through or the changes that her body was going through. Nor did I know she had to run to the bathroom and get sick before she could even say good morning.

I thought that I was crowding her and that she needed space. So that's what I gave her. When she needed me most, I left her home with her electronic devices to keep her busy and went on with my day, thinking she was okay at home. One day, when she was snapping like usual, I got up and told her I would be back. When I started out the door, she called my name. I could tell by her voice that she was fighting back the tears.

"I really need your help!" she said as tears began to flow down her pretty little face. "I feel like I am going through this pregnancy by myself, Alex."

Guilt washed over me, and I pulled her to my chest, hugged her, and apologized. From that moment on, I made a conscious effort to be more engaged and help-ful. I started to rub her feet without her asking. Sometimes I would surprise her by doing the grocery shopping and coming home early to cook her dinner. I would even bring a flower or two home for her sometimes.

When I began to get into the game, she played the game better too. She brightened up and was truly happier and less stressed. Just as I would surprise her sometimes, she would also start doing little things for me. The game finally took a turn, and we were winning again. As the pregnancy progressed, we both became very excited. The game is so much more exciting when both players show up.

Now it is time to shift gears and focus on the physical changes that occur during the first trimester of pregnancy. We will take a journey together to learn how your baby is developing and what your partner is going through and prepare you for doctor appointments, the big game day, and fatherhood. Knowing these things will help you support your partner and be the best father you can be.

4

OPENING KICK-OFF: THE FIRST TRIMESTER

Oh, the joys of the first trimester of pregnancy.....said no woman ever!

— UNKNOWN

Welcome to the wild ride of the first trimester of pregnancy. I know it's your first time going through this, and it can be a bit overwhelming. Don't worry, though; I got your back. You have learned a little about pregnancy, and now it is time to put some things we learned into action while we learn some more.

You have braced and prepared yourself for this pregnancy. You have decided to be on this team, and you will give it your best shot. Your best shot is all you got, and, believe me, it is all you will need. If you put in the work and take the time to learn, you will be well on your way to winning the big game you have been waiting nine months for.

In this chapter, I will give you the lowdown and nitty gritty on what is happening with your little one and how your superstar is developing in Mommy's belly. You will see all the work your little superstar and your partner have put in during these weeks to get ready for the big game day–the birth of your first child.

I'm going to help you ensure you are prepared for this trimester by letting you know how your baby-to-be is developing, cluing you in on your partner's symptoms and journey, and preparing you for this trimester's doctor visits. It will seem like a lot to take in, and I'm not going to sugarcoat it for you. Don't worry; it's not all doom and gloom. There will be plenty of fun, exciting things that will be happening too.

You first should know just how long pregnancy is. The total length of pregnancy is 40 weeks and is divided into the first, second, and third trimesters. The first trimester lasts from month one of pregnancy to the end of the third month. The second trimester will begin at month four and will end at the end of month six. The third trimester will start at the beginning of month seven and end at the end of month nine.

It does seem unreal that you can carry a baby for 40 weeks. That's a long time to carry extra weight around your waist, but it's all worth it. When your little bundle of joy comes into this world, both you and your partner will finally see what it feels like to love another human being with all your heart.

The first trimester of pregnancy is an important one. Sometimes, it is the make or break in determining whether the pregnancy will be normal or high-risk. Miscarriages happen the most at this stage of pregnancy, so it is crucial that you and your partner follow all the doctor's orders. This is not the time to stress your partner out, either. It would be best to ensure other people didn't stress her out also.

PREGNANCY PLAYBOOK

Congratulations, you are going to be a father. Many cool things are taking place in your partner's body right now. However, the two of you do not know it yet. This is about to be a fast, fun, emotional journey. It will also be an exciting one too. So, let's dive into it and look at what is happening in this first month of pregnancy for your growing superstar and your partner.

Weeks 1 through 4

Your Growing Superstar

The embryo has made quite a journey so far. As just a tiny, teeny egg, it bursts through the defense of the fallopian tubes. Then, it was tackled by the sperm cell as it tried to rush into the uterus. The sperm and egg became tangled up together after the sperm "tackled" the egg. Still tangled up and stuck together, they both scored a touchdown in the uterus, where it will stay for the next nine months as it develops into your little superstar. Your baby has officially been conceived, although neither of you knows it yet.

So far, your growing little superstar has made the following developments:

- The ball of cells begins to form layers and fluid-filled sacs.
- The earliest part of afterbirth has already started to develop.
- Your little superstar has grown and is now officially known as an embryo.

- A tube that will soon grow into the embryo's brain and spinal cord has grown alongside the embryo's length.
- The heart is now only a tube but begins to beat as your baby grows.
- On the side of the head, simple structures start to form. As time flies by, these simple structures will morph into eyes and ears.
- Little bumps, called limb buds, start forming and will soon become arms and legs.
- In these four weeks, your embryo has reached a millimeter in length.

Momma's Symptoms

Momma isn't having many symptoms quite yet, but she may experience:

- Heightened sense of smell
- Metallic taste in the mouth
- Lower abdomen pressure
- Increased sex drive
- Tender breasts
- Mild cramping
- Missed period
- Increased vaginal discharge

Weeks 5 and 6

Congratulations, you and your partner have made it to the sixth week of pregnancy. Your partner is now one and a half months pregnant. A lot of things are happening this week. Now, pregnancy is about to get exciting.

Your Growing Superstar

Your little superstar in the making will make a lot of progress this week with its growth and development. Here is a look at what changes your baby will have completed by the end of this week:

- Your baby is now the size of an orange seed.
- It has graduated from an embryo to a fetus.
- Placenta has begun to develop and will have developed entirely by the end of this trimester. The placenta is an organ that will soon connect your Fetus to the uterine wall, providing the baby with nutrients and oxygen.
- The ectoderm, also known as the outer layer of skin, is starting to form important structures such as the nervous system, nails, skin, and hair.
- Mesoderm is becoming your little superstar's circulatory system and will develop bones, muscles, and kidneys.

- The gestational sac can now be seen on your ultrasound, confirming your partner's pregnancy.

Momma's Symptoms and Journey

- All symptoms from months before, and they may be getting worse.
- Your partner's breasts are now beginning to prepare for the little one. This month your partner may start to notice changes in her breast.
- Your partner may feel the need to urinate a lot more often.
- Emotions are now starting to run wild. You can help your significant other out by being more understanding, even if you don't have a clue about what she is feeling or going through.
- Mom may now get nauseous when she smells certain things.
- She may begin to feel exhausted.
- Pregnancy hormones have kicked in.
- Bloating will now occasionally occur.
- Morning sickness is probably getting worse (unless she is one of the lucky few who don't get sick during pregnancy).

Mom should:

- If she has not already, take a test because the pregnancy should be monitored by a doctor as soon as possible.
- Mom should take prenatal vitamins and a folic acid supplement.
- Make safe food choices (which will be discussed later)
- Get plenty of rest and try to relax

Mom should not:

- Ride rollercoasters
- Play contact sports
- Smoke cigarettes or marijuana
- Drink alcohol
- Do drugs of any kind
- Get in hot tubes
- Get any tattoos
- Change cat litter

Whistle Blown

- Ectopic pregnancy is dangerous to the mother and child and is also the cause of many miscarriages. An ectopic pregnancy occurs when the fertilized egg implants inside the fallopian tube rather than the uterine wall. These are one of the many reasons why making a doctor's appointment is crucial as soon as you find out you are pregnant.

- You should find a dentist if you do not have one. Your teeth will not get as much calcium now that you are pregnant. Women with gum disease also have a higher chance of getting preeclampsia during pregnancy.

Weeks 7 and 8

Your partner has made it to the two-month mark. Although miscarriage is still very possible, the risk of miscarriage has decreased some. Your baby is growing very fast and making significant changes. Let's take a look at how your baby is developing and the symptoms your partner will have during these two weeks:

Your Growing Superstar

- The Fetus is now ½ inches long
- The Fetus's facial features are more defined
- Arm and leg buds are growing longer
- Eyes are developing
- The Fetus's brain now consists of the forebrain, midbrain, and hindbrain

- The brain is gaining at a rate of 100 cells per minute!
- Lips, nose, and genitals are starting to form
- The Toes are nearly formed.
- Muscles begin to form.
- Intestines are growing rapidly.
- The Fetus now has a four-chambered heart
- The spinal column has developed and can now be seen
- Electrical activity begins in the brain
- Fingers begin to develop
- Blood is being pumped through the umbilical cord to the Fetus
- A bluish amniotic sac surrounds the Fetus now, and the fluid inside will protect the baby until they are born

Momma's Symptoms and Journey

- Sense of smell is heightened
- Change in taste of foods
- Your partner may begin to have strange dreams
- She is probably starting to experience cramping
- She may be experiencing more headaches than usual
- She is more than likely still experiencing nausea as well

- She should still follow all the shoulds and shouldn't that are mentioned above.
- By now, you should have your first doctor's appointment scheduled

Weeks Nine and Ten

It may appear like your growing superstar can't make many changes in just two weeks, but the Fetus has made many changes. Your partner is now 2 ½ months pregnant, and the time to find out the gender of this superstar will be here before you know it. Let's see how your Fetus has changed this week and what your partner may be experiencing:

Your Growing SuperStar

- The Fetus is now 1 ½ inches long
- The Fetus weighs ½ ounce
- The ears have moved to their normal position
- Fetal movements and heartbeat are now able to be detected by an ultrasound
- Glands begin to work
- Kidneys are now functioning and making urine
- Tooth buds are now recognizable
- The head is very large, and it takes up half the Fetus's length
- Fetus now looks like a human

- Have developed small arms, legs, fingers, and toes
- First, bone cells begin to replace cartilage

Momma's Symptoms and Journey

- Still may experience all prior symptoms mentioned
- Breast and nipples are growing, and they are itchy and tender
- Your partner's emotions could be running a little wild right now
- Heartburn may be becoming more frequent and intense
- Constipation might make it difficult for her to go to the bathroom
- Fatigue or other sleep issues might become more intense
- Frequent urination might interrupt your plans

Weeks 11 and 12

Your partner is wrapping up her second month of pregnancy. She will be considered three months pregnant at the end of the 12th week. What's even more exciting? You're over the halfway mark of finding out the gender of your baby. Although we can't tell just yet the gender of your little one, it has developed a lot. Your partner has also come a long way on this journey, but it's not almost over yet. Let's take a look at how your team is getting ready for the big game day:

Your Growing Superstar

- The Fetus has grown to be 2 ½ inches long this week, the size of nail scissors, and now weighs an ounce.
- The Fetus's head is still enormous and takes up half the baby's body length.
- Taste buds are developing.
- Organs are beginning to take shape inside the Fetus.
- Breathing and fetal movements can now be seen during an ultrasound.
- Although you can't feel it yet, the Fetus can now move its arms and legs.
- The Fetus now has transparent skin.
- Fingernails are forming on their fingers.
- The liver is now working and making red blood cells.

Your Partner's Symptoms and Journey

- Your partner may now be showing the first signs of a baby bump

- Your partner is starting to look more beautiful than ever. Her hair is getting long and thick. No need for her to get her nails done because, boy, are hers getting long and pretty.
- Your partner's skin is glowing and smoothing out.
- Due to her expanding uterus, she needs more than a few bathroom breaks, especially at night. You can help keep her safe by adding night lights that light the way to your partner's restroom in your home. Sometimes pregnant women can be a little clumsy.
- She is still very fatigued.
- She may or may not be feeling up to having intercourse at this moment. However, this doesn't mean there aren't other ways to connect with her. Climb in bed and watch some chick flicks with her, or maybe even a good comedy. Don't you dare climb into bed to watch a movie with her without bringing the snacks!

IMPORTANT DOCTOR VISITS AND TESTS THIS TRIMESTER

On your journey, you and your partner will become good friends with your chosen OB-GYN, who will be the coach of this pregnancy. During the first trimester, you will see the doctor once a month. Although you will not have very many doctor appointments this trimester, many important things will take place at the appointments you do have. Below you will find out what will happen at your most crucial first-trimester doctor appointments:

First Doctor's Visit

When: Your first doctor's visit will take place between weeks 5-10 of pregnancy. Basically, the sooner you know your partner is pregnant, the sooner the doctor's visit will occur. When your partner finds out she is pregnant, she should call an OB-GYN she trusts to coach her pregnancy.

What Will Take Place: Try not to get overwhelmed at the first appointment. There will be a lot that will take place at this appointment. Most doctor offices suggest that you arrive 15 minutes prior to your appointment time. At this appointment, they will:

- Confirm your partner's pregnancy.
- Want to discuss your, your partner's, and both of your family's medical history, so it is important that you attend this visit.
- Your partner will be given a pap smear to make sure everything down under is working correctly and free of STDs. This is very

important because, if STDs are present, they will need to be taken care of before the baby is born so they are not passed from mother to child. Most STDs are very easy to get rid of if you take the medication as directed. Don't worry; you will not have to be in the room for this part.

- Schedule your partner for genetic screenings. Two types of genetic testing can be done to see if your baby will have genetic disorders. The two tests are Cell-free Fetal DNA testing, which tests for conditions caused by abnormal numbers of chromosomes, and Chorionic Villus sampling, or CVS. During a CVS test, a tissue sample will be taken from the placenta to test for genetic disorders. The choice to have these tests done is up to you. If you prefer not to, you do not have to have DNA testing done.

- Test your partner's urine to ensure there aren't any signs of a urinary tract infection.

- Provide you and your partner with the first ultrasound of your little growing superstar. The ultrasound will be done to check the Fetus's heartbeat and measure the baby. You will also get your due date. (The baby's heartbeat is not detectable until the sixth or seventh week. It's best to wait till this time to schedule the appointment).

- Discuss vaginal bleeding during pregnancy and give you a long list of do's and don'ts during pregnancy. It is important that your partner follow these recommendations so that she and the baby stay happy and healthy.

The doctor will draw your partner's blood, and it will be tested for the following:

- Blood type (in case there is a need for blood transfusion at the time of birth)
- Blood count to test for anemia and signs of infection or illness
- Immunity to rubella
- Hepatitis B
- HIV
- Syphilis

Doctor's Visit Number Two

When: The second doctor's appointment should occur anywhere between the 10th and 13th weeks of pregnancy.

What Will Take Place: The purpose of this appointment will be to check on your partner and how she is feeling. The doctor will discuss her symptoms and offer help with her symptoms if needed. You will also go over all your lab work and results. At every appointment, now and in the future, you will get to hear your little one's heartbeat. If an ultrasound to confirm pregnancy was not done at the last visit, it would be done during this one.

This will wrap up the first trimester's journey through pregnancy. In the next chapter, we will jump right into the second trimester. The second trimester is the trimester everyone loves.

Help other new dads master fatherhood with confidence and be their partner's strongest source of support during pregnancy and beyond.

"Only by giving are you able to receive more than you already have."

— *JIM ROHN*

Earlier in this book, I mentioned how the first moments after you realize you are about to be a dad are exhilarating, nerve-wracking, and a little anxiety-inducing, all at once.

When you share the great news with others, a barrage of congratulatory messages and well wishes come your way. Many will have opinions on everything from what type of birth to opt for to the best brands of carriages and baby devices.

But what most people don't talk about are the things that fill you with doubt and worry at nighttime. As you face the fact that your life will be changed irrevocably by the arrival of a little baby, you wonder if you will know how to support your partner during each trimester and the delivery.

You wonder if you will ace tasks like bathing your newborn, changing diapers, and surviving the many emotions that you can experience once your child is born.

Financial concerns may also run through your head. Will you need to make changes to your current work schedule, and if so, how will the bills get paid?

I mentioned that my own dad wasn't around much when I was young and commended you for wanting to know all about your partner's pregnancy and ways you can be their very best source of support. I wrote this book for anyone who wants to be a confident, informed, proactive first-time father because I know the big difference this can make in your child's life.

You already know how to overcome many of the insecurities that can stump new dads—from questions about sex during pregnancy to how to be your partner's "hype man," and all the doctor visits and tests you will encounter during your partner's first and second trimesters.

If you have found even the slightest of comfort and relief from your stress and worries so far, then you can help other new dads in your position to achieve the same by sharing the knowledge that became your sturdy support.

By leaving a review of this book on Amazon, you'll help countless first-time dads see how vital it is to take a proactive role in their future child's life, from the moment they find out their partner is expecting.

Simply by telling others how this book has helped you and what they can expect to find inside, you'll help them understand that fatherhood is one of the most exhilarating rides they will ever take in life—and the magic never ends.

Scan this QR code to leave a review!

5

FIRST DOWN: THE SECOND TRIMESTER

When I thought I had not yet accomplished anything extraordinary in life, I looked over at my five-month-pregnant wife and knew, right then, that the thought I had was nothing more than a lie. I got the most beautiful woman in the world pregnant. I created a family, and there is nothing better that I could ever accomplish.

— UNKNOWN

Congratulations, your partner has made it to the fun stage of pregnancy: the second trimester! Your partner is now four months pregnant. The second trimester of pregnancy includes pregnancy months four, five, and six. During this trimester, so many exciting things will happen for both your growing superstar and your partner.

The great thing about the second trimester is that it is usually considered the most comfortable trimester of pregnancy. Typically morning sickness fades away, and those little kicks and movements from the baby are not very strong yet. This trimester you and your partner should take a deep breath and enjoy the pregnancy and each other.

This is also when you should begin to get to know your baby and let them know you are their daddy. Your baby will do so much development this trimester, and many changes will occur with your partner. That said, let's look at what will be going on these next three months.

PREGNANCY PLAYBOOK

Weeks 13-14

Your baby has made it a long way. It is now a four-month-old fetus and is developing very fast. By the end of week 14, your Fetus will have made the following developments:

Your Growing Superstar

- The Fetus is now the size of a pickle
- Fetus's length is 3 ½ inches long
- Sex organs are almost fully developed
- The Fetus can now suck its thumb
- Inside the sac, the Fetus will now urinate
- The baby's fingerprints are developing
- A thin fuzzy layer of hair called lanugo will begin to cover the Fetus to protect its skin

Momma's Symptoms and Journey

- Mom may now start to feel better
- She will feel less nauseous
- Momma's appetite is increasing
- She may get frequent UTIs and yeast infections due to increased vaginal discharge.
- Each week, momma will gain about a pound or more a week from here on out
- Her gums may bleed when brushing her teeth due to increased blood flow
- She will begin to feel more energetic
- Surprisingly, she may be dealing with nasal congestion even though she doesn't have a cold.

- Your partner may have an increased sex drive, so you might as well get comfortable with intercourse during pregnancy.
- She may begin to experience round ligament pain around her hips

Weeks 15-16

Your Growing Superstar

- Fetus is now 5-6 inches long
- Fetus is the size of a doughnut by the end of week 16
- Taste buds are fully developed
- Fetus can now make facial expressions
- Your Fetus can now hear and enjoy it when you speak to them. Now is the time to let that baby hear their father's voice. Talk to your partner's belly; the baby will remember your voice when they're born.
- If you are having a girl, her ovaries are now making their own millions of little tiny eggs.
- The Fetus has developed eyelashes and eyebrows.

Momma's Symptoms and Journey

- Momma's tendons and muscles are beginning to relax as they prepare for childbirth. This may cause your partner a little bit of back pain.
- Your partner's breasts are getting larger and fuller.
- Mom may experience some constipation still.
- Her skin is getting even more beautiful and glowing even more than before.
- Falls are common during this time due to the shift in body weight. It is a great idea for your partner to wear flat shoes, hold on to handrails, and be careful when she gets up to use the restroom in the middle of the night.

Weeks 17-18

Your Growing Superstar

- Your little baby is now a whopping 5 ½ inches long at the end of week 18.
- The Fetus is now the size of a cupcake.
- Your little one can now taste whatever mom eats and may even respond to what it likes that she eats.

- This is the week I'm sure you have all been waiting for. The gender of your little superstar can now be determined!

Momma's Symptoms and Journey

- Momma is starting to feel hungry all the time as her appetite increases.
- Your partner's breasts and belly are growing rapidly. All the stretching of her skin may cause her skin to be a little itchy.
- She is still rocking that beautiful pregnancy glow to the fullest.
- Now is a good time to go ahead and talk about how you will manage when the baby comes. Who will do middle-of-the-night feedings? When will Mom get to rest? What doctor will you take your little one to? Etc.
- Your partner's uterus is the size of a cantaloupe.
- She may feel dizzy or faint at times. If so, encourage her to sit down and rest. Encourage her to also speak to her doctor.

Weeks 19-20

Your Growing Superstar

- Your baby's movements are increasing and can be felt outside of the momma's belly.
- The Fetus is now about 7 inches long.
- Your little one is the size of a slice of bread.
- The Fetus's muscles are growing.
- The Fetus is now doing acrobatics inside the uterus.

Momma's Symptoms and Journey

- Your partner is probably experiencing hip and groin pain.
- She may have a hard time finding a comfortable position to sleep in. Full-body pregnancy pillows may help with this issue.
- Some women start getting brown spots on their faces around this time. Don't worry; these spots will fade after your partner gives birth.
- If you already have a will drawn up, now would be a good time to update it. Now would be the best time to make one if you don't. You would want to put in your will who should raise your child if something happens to you and your partner.

- Many women begin planning their baby showers now.
- Your partner may start to feel more energetic.
- Momma may have increased yeast infections due to increased vaginal discharge.
- She is starting to gain weight, but that is perfectly normal and fine.

Weeks 21-22

Your Growing Superstar

- At the end of week 22, your baby-to-be will be 10 ½ inches long and the size of a tiny doll baby.
- The Fetus now weighs one pound.
- The Fetus's movements have been increasing and are more coordinated.
- The Fetus is now practicing swallowing by drinking amniotic fluid.
- Your little superstar in the making's muscles are developing and getting stronger, and so is their ability to see and hear.
- If your partner had to deliver the baby this week for an emergency, your little one now has a great chance of surviving.

Momma's Symptoms and Journey

- Stretch marks are now popping up all over your partner's body; some will disappear after delivery.
- You and your partner can now feel the Fetus move and kick in her belly.
- Your partner's feet may be beginning to swell.
- Bloating is expected at this time, as well as gas.
- Heartburn is in full force.
- Leg cramps may disrupt sleep.

Weeks 23-24

Your Growing Superstar

- Your little one now weighs two pounds and is nine inches long.
- Your baby will be the size of a pomegranate by the end of week 24.
- The Fetus is now able to blink its little eyelids.
- Fat is now starting to be stored under the Fetus's skin.
- Your baby-to-be can now suck not just their thumb but also their fingers and hands.
- Your baby can hear very well now. It is an excellent time to talk to your baby and, even

better, play some music. Your partner may feel the baby start dancing when they hear the beat.

Momma's Symptoms and Journey

- Momma may start feeling "fuzzy" minded.
- Her feet are still swelling.
- Your partner may get heat rashes easily.
- She may still be experiencing skin discoloration.
- Bloating and gas are still hanging around.
- Your partner may nod off a lot more. Who can blame her? She is growing a baby inside of her body. Who wouldn't be tired?

Weeks 25-26

Your Growing Superstar

- Your baby is now 14+ inches long and weighs three or more pounds.
- Your little one should be doing all the things it has done thus far.
- Room is beginning to get a little cramped in Mommy's belly. Your partner will really feel all the Fetus's jabs and kicks now, and you will be able to see them and feel them too.

Momma's Symptoms and Journey

- Your partner is now wrapping up her second trimester of pregnancy and moving into her seventh month of pregnancy.
- The big day is approaching, and it's coming very fast. Now is the time to make sure you have your baby shower planned and attend any classes you would like to attend.
- Your partner may now suffer from insomnia. If your partner is one of the women who do suffer from insomnia, encourage her to speak with her doctor. There are things her OB-GYN may be able to do to help her out with this.

IMPORTANT DOCTOR'S VISITS AND TESTS THIS TRIMESTER

Your partner will have more doctor's appointments in the second trimester than she did in the first three months. Soon, instead of once a month, she will be seen every other week. At every doctor's appointment, they will check the mother's uterus size and listen to your baby's heartbeat. They will also be checking her weight, blood pressure, and urine at every appointment. If additional tests are needed, they will also draw blood.

In the second trimester, there are a few tests that are considered optional; however, there are tests that are considered mandatory. Below, you will find the weeks of important tests that are done in the second trimester and the reasoning behind them:

Timing of Appointment	Test That Will be Done	Information About Tests and Procedures to be Done
Weeks 15-18	Alpha-fetoprotein screening	This optional test draws the mother's blood to test for fetal spinal cord abnormalities.
Weeks 20	Gender Ultrasound	The moment most of you have been waiting for. You can now find out if you are having a girl or boy.
Weeks 24-28	-Anemia screen -Glucose tolerance test	-Anemia screen test for low levels of iron -The glucose tolerance test for gestational diabetes. She will need to fast for this test. If your partner has hypoglycemia, let her provider know so the right precautions can be taken for the glucose tolerance test.

This will wrap up the second trimester. We are now going to slide into the final stage: the third trimester. By now, the baby is really starting to bulk up and settle into a head-down position as they get ready to be caught by the coach. Let's not forget that your partner is now feeling the pain and pressure in more ways than one. Now is the time for you, Dad, to step up and get all into the game. Your partner is really going to need you in the final quarter of the game–more than she has before.

6

TOUCHDOWN: THE THIRD TRIMESTER

She is in the final push of the playoffs and about to score the biggest touchdown ever......and I am her biggest fan.

— ANONYMOUS

I t is almost time to meet your new little superstar. Your partner is now seven months along and only has two more months to go. This trimester, your baby is almost fully developed. Now, they will begin to get ready for delivery.

This is the home stretch, the final countdown, and the clock is steadily ticking down. You will finally get to meet the incredible little human you have been waiting for at the end of this quarter. And let me tell you, the third trimester is one exciting adventure you do not want to miss. It's a time of excitement, anticipation, nervousness, thrills, and bonding between you, your partner, and, yes, even the baby baking in your partner's uterus.

Your partner will go through more changes than your baby will this trimester. You both will make sure that everything is in order and ready to go for delivery. Now you will be having your baby shower and be able to get a tally of what other items your baby may need. This trimester is an exciting stage in pregnancy, so let's look at what's going on with your baby and partner this trimester.

PREGNANCY PLAYBOOK

Weeks 28-30

Your Growing Superstar

- Your baby's eyes can now completely open.
- Your baby's eyelashes are fully formed.
- The baby's central nervous system can direct rhythmic breathing movements.

- Baby is now putting on about half a pound a week.
- Space in the amniotic sac is limited, and the baby feels cramped.
- Your little one may be one of the lucky babies born with a head full of hair.
- Red blood cells are forming in your little one's bone marrow.
- By the end of week 30, your baby will be around 15 inches long and weigh about 3 ½ pounds.

Momma's Symptoms and Journey

- Mom may have an increase in blood pressure now.
- Colostrum may leak from the mom's breast due to the beginning of milk production.
- Mom may feel "heavy-bellied" and uncomfortable due to her growing uterus.

Weeks 31-34

Your Growing Superstar

- Your baby has finished most of its development and will prepare for birth.

- Your baby is now putting on fat to keep them warm.
- Your baby's bones are hardening.
- Baby is now practicing breathing.
- The lanugo hair that once covered your baby is now falling off its body.
- Your baby will be around 12-13 inches long and weigh about 4 ½ pounds by week 34.

Momma's Symptoms and Journey

- Stretch marks may now be more visible and pronounced.
- Mom may begin to feel tightening and hardening near the uterus. These are contractions known as Braxton Hicks contractions.

Weeks 35-37

Your Growing Superstar

- Your baby now has a firm grasp.
- Baby is running out of room in the uterus.
- Your baby will now start descending into the pelvis.
- The doctor will now check to see if the baby is in a breech position.

Momma's Symptoms and Journey

- During these weeks, mom may go into a nesting stage. She may begin cleaning the house from top to bottom, preparing for the baby's big arrival.
- Mom may lose her mucus plug, also known as "bloody show," during these weeks.
- Mom may begin to feel very uncomfortable as the baby descends into the pelvic region.
- Her pregnant belly looks like it has dropped, and that's because it probably has. This happens as the baby moves down into the pelvic region.

Weeks 38-40

- Your baby is now ready to enter the world any minute.
- By the end of week 40, your baby will be around 20 inches long and will weigh about 7 ½ pounds.

Momma's Symptoms and Journey

- This is it; the baby can be born at any time now.
- Your partner's cervix is now dilating to prepare for birth.

- Your partner's water will break, or the doctor will schedule her to induce labor.
- Your baby enters the world after such a long journey through pregnancy.
- Congratulations! You are now a father by the end of the 40th week–unless pregnancy goes over a week or so.

IMPORTANT DOCTOR'S VISITS AND TESTS THIS TRIMESTER

During the third trimester, your partner will see her doctor every two weeks until week 36. After week 36, your partner will see the doctor once a week for the remainder of her pregnancy. Even though she will see the doctor more this trimester, the most crucial tests and other important things have already occurred.

Just as the doctor did in all the prior visits, the doctor will continue to check the Mother's uterine size and listen to your baby's heart rate. The doctor will also continue to check your partner's urine, weight, and blood pressure. The doctor will also make sure that your partner is feeling fine. Near the end of pregnancy, the doctor will also check to see if the baby is in a breech position.

At week 36, your partner will be given a group beta strep culture. This test checks for the presence of GBS in pregnant women. If the test is positive, your partner will need antibiotics during labor. Your partner will also discuss pain relief for labor and delivery with their doctor.

Most women choose to have an epidural. This pain relief option helps numbs most, if not all, of the pain and discomfort a woman feels during the stages of labor if it works. I know a woman where this pain relief procedure only worked on one-half of her body. When she was given something else to try to ease the pain, she said it felt like her body was on fire. Make sure you discuss all options with your partner's healthcare provider with your partner to make sure she is as safe as she can be during labor and delivery.

Sometimes, a woman never loses her plug, and her water doesn't break. She will go over her 40th week of pregnancy and wonder why she hasn't had this baby yet. Many women will try to induce labor themselves, which is perfectly fine. They may want to have sex, dance their butts off, do squats, walk, and even drink castor oil to try and induce their labor. Sometimes these things work, but most of the time, they don't.

If your partner hits the 41-week mark, your doctor will prepare to serve the baby an eviction notice or, in other words, induce labor. When and if necessary to induce labor, the doctor will schedule a day for your partner to have the baby. Most women prefer this because it takes away a lot of labor fears. If your partner is being induced, she cannot eat or drink anything 12 hours before arriving at the hospital.

When she arrives at the hospital, the doctor will come in and break her water after she is settled in. This will make contractions begin. The doctor will wait until your partner can no longer manage the contractions before an anesthesiologist is called in to give her an epidural. Sometimes the OB-GYN will provide other forms of pain relief until your partner has reached a particular stage or amount of dilation before prescribing an epidural, as the medication can slow down labor.

You have finally made it to the end of pregnancy. Now it's time for the big game. The game we all have been waiting for. Your new teammate will soon enter the world any minute now. Aren't you so excited?

GAME TIME

T he day you have all been waiting for so dang long is finally here. It's finally the big day. Soon your baby will be here. You can finally hold the baby you have been counting down for. *It's finally game time!*

I have a friend who delivered on her family's favorite team's big game day. My friend Linda is from Georgia, and every member of her family is a diehard Georgia Bulldogs fan. They are also diehard new baby fans. I don't know what the doctor was thinking nor why he scheduled to induce labor on the same day as the Georgia Bulldogs' first season game, but he did. Then again, Linda didn't care much for college football and couldn't wait to meet her baby, so it could have been her doing.

When Linda's Family is about to welcome a baby into the world, the whole family waits at the hospital for the baby to enter the world. Her family is not the quiet type of family either. Nope, they are loud Southerners who like to joke and pick at each other. However, on this day, the men in Linda's Family were not too happy about sitting up at the hospital to welcome the baby into the world on this particular day. All she heard all day was her family asking her when she would spit that baby out.

They would make sure she knew they had a game to get home to watch, and the clock was ticking. One by one, the men would send each other back to her room to tell her to hurry up and have the baby. First, her dad came into her delivery room, trying to rush her to have a baby. After she kicked her father out, she kicked her child's father out for laughing at her dad and for being her dad's hype man.

Not even 20 minutes after kicking her child's father and dad out of the room, her Uncle Shane brought his behind into her room too. Now, her uncle Shane was only about five years older than she was, and her father raised him because their Mother died when he was a teenager. In other words, he has always been more of an aggravating big brother to her than an uncle.

THE COMPLETE PREGNANCY GUIDE FOR MEN | 101

"Man, you ain't had that baby yet?" She squinted her eyes at Shane like she wanted to tackle him if she could. Her threatening looks didn't scare that red-headed uncle of hers, though, because he kept right on running his mouth.

"I told you months ago that I had a game to watch tonight. I tell you this every freaking year. Your freaking water ain't even broken yet. That's how I know you and the doctor scheduled to induce," he chuckled and shook his head before finishing his little rant. "This game has probably been planned longer than you have even been pregnant. But, only two days ago, the bright doctor scheduled you to be induced because you are a scaredy cat." That's when the doctor walked into the room.

A smile spread across Shane's face. She knew right then and there that he was going to embarrass her. She was glad the doctor knew Shane from delivering his two girls. "Doctor! Just the man I wanted to see. I have a question for you."

"Good to see you again, Shane. What's your question? Hold on, let me guess, will the baby be here before the game starts?" he laughed.

Shane chuckled and shook his head no. "You scheduled this baby to come today just a few days ago. You all could have picked yesterday. You all could have picked tomorrow. But what day did you all pick, huh? You all picked *game day*! Not only game day but the first game of the season. Dr. Nevin, what were you thinking? You weren't thinking at all, were you?" He thought he got the doctor, but he must have forgotten that Dr. Nevin had a few tricks and jokes up his sleeve too.

"I was thinking alright. I thought this out very well too. I made sure I scheduled it right when she wanted it because I got off work regardless of whether this little man had made his grand entrance or not. That's what I'm coming to tell her now. I induced her 16 hours ago, and that baby does not want to come out, so," he looked at Linda, "if you want me to deliver this baby, then you better tell it to hurry up. I'm leaving here in enough time to watch the kickoff from my recliner. If Elijah is not out here in 45 minutes, Dr. House will deliver the baby."

They all looked at the doctor, and he laughed; then, they all laughed. Then, the doctor kicked Shane out of the room because Linda started feeling a lot of pressure and pain, so he wanted to check how things were progressing. Her epidural didn't work on her right side. When the doctor checked if the baby was coming, the doctor told Shane's wife, who was still in the room, to hurry up and get the baby's father and Linda's Mother from the waiting room. The baby was coming out right now. He hollered for the nurses and then shouted down the hall one last time at Shane's wife, *"You might wanna run! This baby is ready."* Her mom and the child's dad flew into the room just in time. It was time to start pushing. Her aunt held one leg, the child's daddy had another, and her Mother snapped photo after photo.

She pushed and screamed, screamed and pushed. Then, the baby just shot right out. Her son blasted into this world 15 minutes before Georgia's first kickoff of the season. Linda had her healthy baby boy on Game Day.

Osho once said, "The moment a baby is born, the Mother is also born. She never existed before." These words ring true, not just for mothers but for fathers too. The moment a baby is born, the father is also transformed into the type of man he has never been before. The experience of childbirth has the power to change both parents for the better in ways neither of them ever thought was possible.

BIRTHING OPTIONS

I bet you thought the only way to have a baby was at the hospital. If you thought this, let me say you're wrong. Don't worry; I was also shocked when I learned that women have birthing options. They can if they want to return to the good old days and have a baby at home. They can have the baby in the bathtub if they want to be new, hip, and creative! Who knew, right? Well, you are about to be up-to-date. I have done my research, and you are about to learn your partner's options for giving birth to your new teammate.

Before we enter labor and delivery in the hospital, I will briefly discuss other birthing options. For starters, some women are not able to have natural births. When this occurs, women are given a cesarean birth, which most people call a c-section. A c-section is a surgical procedure to deliver a baby when a vaginal delivery can't be done safely.

A c-section allows the baby to be delivered through incisions in your partner's abdomen and uterus. The doctor will usually know ahead of time if she will need to have your baby by c-section and will schedule a date to operate. Sometimes, a woman goes into labor and expects to have the baby naturally but ends up needing a C-section. This happens when something isn't going right when trying to deliver a baby naturally. Unplanned c-sections may occur if:

- Labor is prolonged.
- The umbilical cord gets looped around the baby's neck or body. This can be extremely

dangerous and is the cause of many fetal deaths at birth.
- The placenta separates from the wall of the uterus before the baby is born.
- If the fetus is in distress.
- When your baby is in a breech position.
- If your partner's water has been broken for over 24 hours

From start to finish, the surgery usually takes about 45 minutes. The incisions that are made in the wall of your uterus are around 3-4 inches. After the baby is delivered, the doctor will then deliver the placenta. Once both the baby and placenta have been delivered, the doctor will stitch your partner's uterus and close the incision he has made in their abdomen using either stitches or staples. Your partner will be sore for several days, so she will have a more extended hospital stay if she has a C-section. They will also make sure that she has pain medication for her discomfort at home.

Once home, if your partner notices any of the following, she should call her doctor:

- Red or swollen incision.
- Pus or any other fluid leaking from the incision location.
- If she has a fever or any worsening pain.

- If she is experiencing heavy bleeding, severe pelvic pain, and cramping.

Full recovery from a c-section takes about six to eight weeks. Before having intercourse, you should speak to your partner's healthcare provider about when trying is okay. Every woman is different and heals at different paces.

C-sections and natural hospital births are not very exciting for women in labor. Let's look at a birthing option that is the coolest thing I have ever heard of. That birthing option is a *water birth*! Yes, you heard me right; women can choose to give birth in water. Why is this so cool to me? Only because I am a big believer that warm baths can take any pain in the world away.

Water birth is just what it says. It's the process of having your child delivered in a tub of warm water. According to the Corpus Christi Birthing Center (2017), "The theory behind water birth is that since the baby has already been in the amniotic fluid sac for nine months, birthing in a similar environment is gentler and less stressful for the mother."

There are so many benefits to choosing to have a water birth, such as (CCBC, 2017):

- Warm water tends to be very soothing, relaxing, and comforting during this time of stress and anxiety.
- When women labor in warm water, it has been shown to increase their energy, which they will need when it is time to push.
- Warm water relieves pain. No matter what type of pain you have, warm water will at least alleviate it to a certain degree.
- Buoyancy improves your partner's blood circulation.
- Water births reduce women's anxiety and fears of giving birth.

Just like all birthing options, water births do have a few risks. The water could enter the Mother's bloodstream and cause a water embolism. Though the British Medical Journal is 95% confident in the safety of water births, they see a possible risk of water aspiration (CCBC, 2017). There is a risk of the baby gasping for air if the umbilical cord gets twisted or kinked during delivery. If this happens, the baby could inhale water. However, this situation is extremely rare since the baby usually does not inhale until they are exposed to air. All

---

in all, water births do tend to be very safe options and more comforting.

However, water births are not for everyone. Below is a table of situations that are not ideal for water births:

Conditions Not Ideal for Water Birth	Reason Why
If you have herpes	Herpes transfers very easily in water. Discuss this risk with your doctor if you want a water birth and have been diagnosed with herpes.
If your baby is breech	Water births can be done with babies in the breech position, but there are risks that you should speak with your healthcare provider about before deciding to have a water birth for a baby in the breech position.
Preterm labor is expected.	Water is not recommended for those expected to be in preterm labor.
Severe Meconium	You may still be able to have a water birth if there is meconium. In this case, you will be helped to lift your pelvis out of the water to birth the infant. Discussing your options with your partner's healthcare provider prior is always best.
If you have toxemia or preeclampsia	The risk for these conditions should be discussed thoroughly with your partner's healthcare provider.

The best thing about water birth is that there is no extra cost if this is what you decide to do. Depending on your location and doctor's office, some hospitals have birthing tubs available. You could also choose to do it at home on your own. Make it a party if you want to. Your partner and select family members can even get in the birthing tub with you. If you would like to do a home water birth but don't have a birthing tub lying around, which most people don't, you can rent one online for about $350. If your partner is interested in water birth, tell her to speak with her provider, and they will get her all set up and ready to deliver the baby in the water.

Home birth is also an option for mothers. The home birth option involves the participation of one or more trained midwives and is only ideal for low-risk pregnancies (CCBC, 2017). Many women prefer to have a baby at home because that is where they are more comfortable.

In your home, your partner is free to move around, change positions, take showers to help relieve the pain and eat and drink freely during labor. She won't be able to consume anything at the hospital until that baby is out. They will only let her have hard candy and ice chips to suck on.

Home births are not ideal for women who have diabetes, have chronic high blood pressure, or experienced preterm labor. We know home is where your partner feels comfortable, but right now, the safety of your partner and the baby should be the primary concern.

If, at any time, during home labor, your partner feels that she wants to go to the hospital, that is okay. You may take her to the hospital at any time if she chooses to do that. Sometimes the pain gets too much, or the woman will feel exhausted, which is especially common with first-time pregnancies. Midwives may also decide to transfer the Mother to the hospital if there are complications.

LABOR AND DELIVERY

Before we get into the technical stuff about labor and delivery, you should know the signs that indicate that your partner is going into labor. There are two main ways to tell your partner is in labor. Leading up to the two main signs of labor, your partner may notice some signs that she is about to go into labor, such as:

- Braxton Hick contractions
- The baby drops, which means that her belly literally looks as if it dropped down
- Dilation of the cervix
- Cramps
- Back pain
- Loose feeling joints
- Diarrhea

Pregnant women also go through a unique phase called "nesting" when they are nearing labor. The nesting stage is really cool because not only human mothers do this, but also animal mothers. Before labor begins, pregnant mothers get an urge to babyproof their nest.

In this phase of pregnancy, mothers will clean an already cleaned nursery, get hospital bags ready, baby proof and clean the whole house from top to bottom, and make sure that everything in their home is in order. Nesting is a natural mother instinct in all-female species.

If you have a natural childbirth, your baby has to position themselves the correct way so they can safely make their grand entrance into this world. Not all babies need to place themselves in the right way, though. When this happens, the doctor will attempt to turn the baby during a doctor's appointment or before delivery.

The correct way for the baby to position themselves for birth is with their spine against the momma's spine and head toward the cervix. If they are feet toward the cervix, they are in a breech position, which we will discuss more in a moment.

Before the actual labor begins, your partner will experience practice contractions called "Braxton Hicks contractions." The practice contractions begin around weeks 35-37 of pregnancy. Although uncomfortable, they are nowhere near as painful as real contractions.

Two main things can confirm that your partner is in labor if she has a natural birth. The first thing that may happen is your partner may lose her mucus plug. Most people call this the "bloody show." The other thing that can happen is the rupturing of the amniotic sac. Yes, this means her water broke. What do you do if your partner's water breaks? Well, you get her to the hospital as fast as you can.

Once her water breaks, things begin to get real. Contractions–real contractions–start coming in waves. The best thing for your partner to do until getting to the hospital is to try and ride the wave as if she were on a surfboard. True labor contractions progress not only in frequency but also in duration and intensity too.

When your partner experiences contractions, it is because her uterine muscles are shortening to prepare for childbirth. They may start out feeling like achy period cramps. As minutes go by, the cramps get very intense, her belly gets extremely tight, and she also feels excruciating lower back pain. Once you make it to the hospital, they can help relieve the pain caused by the contractions.

Some women have to be scheduled for a c-section if pregnancy complications occur. As discussed earlier, a c-section is when the doctor makes an incision in your lower abdomen to get the baby out of the Mother's belly. Some women's water never breaks, and they have to be induced. In pregnancy, when a woman is induced, that means that the doctor has scheduled a day to break the woman's water to create contractions, which will dilate the cervix.

Some women try to induce themselves, which is normal and perfectly okay. Not to mention, some things a woman will do to get her baby out are fun to watch. My wife tried almost everything. If your partner is nearing this big game day and her water has still not broken, then she could try inducing her labor by:

- Having sex
- Taking a walk
- Doing squats
- Scrubbing the floors
- Exercising
- Dancing
- Eating spicy foods

Now that we know what to look for let's look at what happens when labor starts. Did you know there are actually stages to labor? Yes, there are three labor stages, each helping your partner's body prepare to deliver the baby safely. Below you will find information about each stage of labor:

Stage One: Latent (Early Stage)

The first stage of labor is often referred to as the early stage. This state takes place when labor first begins.

During this labor stage, the body dilates the cervix so the baby can enter through the birthing canal. At first, this stage consists of irregular contractions every 5-30 minutes, which will dilate the cervix up to three centimeters. Next, the contractions will be more intense and occur every 3-5 minutes. Each episode in this phase will last around a minute. This set of contractions will dilate the cervix up to six centimeters.

Once her cervix reaches six centimeters, she will begin the active stage of this stage of pregnancy. This is when her water breaks, and contractions get unbearably intense. Contractions during the active part of this stage of pregnancy will last around 90 seconds.

The whole first stage of pregnancy lasts around 20 long hours. That is a long time to be in pain, and we are only in the first stage. When you end this stage of pregnancy, your partner will have dilated enough to have the baby.

Stage Two: Pushing Stage

The second stage of labor is the pushing stage. Before your partner even attempts to push that baby out, the baby has to be in the correct position. This stage of pregnancy depends on The Three P's:

- *Power:* The forceful uterine contractions that dilate your cervix so your little superstar may pass through.

- *Passenger:* Your little superstar-to-be. As I stated a moment ago, the baby's head should be pointing toward the opening of the cervix to ensure safe delivery. This position is also called the cephalic or head first. When a baby is in breach, their feet will come out first. If this happens, your partner's cervix will not have stretched enough to allow the baby's head and shoulders to come out of the birth canal.

- *Passage*: This is the part we have all waited so long for. After the baby has gotten in the proper position, contractions and your partner will then push the baby downward to the pelvic inlet, where the head of your baby will then pass through the symphysis pubis. From the symphysis pubis, your baby will slide down to the ischial spine, exiting the vagina. Congratulations, you and your partner are now parents! However, labor is not over just yet; we still have one more stage of labor to get through.

Stage Three: Delivery of Placenta

After your partner delivers your baby, there is some-thing else they will have to push out. Your partner now has to deliver the placenta. The uterus will begin contraction again. The placenta will separate from the uterine wall, and your partner will push it out the same way she pushed your child out. A fun, or not-so-fun, fact about the placenta is that some women and men actually keep it and eat it later. The practice of eating the placenta is common in some places overseas.

They say it has very many vitamins and nutrients in it.

Your partner will not be allowed to eat or drink anything during delivery. She will be permitted to have ice chips. If she has a scheduled induction, she will not be allowed to have anything to eat or drink for 12 hours prior to delivery arrival time. Heads up, she will be very hungry after having this baby.

When your partner arrives at the hospital, they will give her an epidural if she has chosen to have one. When they give her the epidural, you must leave the room, Dad. Epidurals are very scary because the needle used for them is extremely long. When they kick you out of the room, a nurse will stay with her while an anesthesiologist administers the epidural, which will be injected into her lower back.

They will be extra careful not to let her see the needle. The nurse will stand before the Mother and ask that she hugs her. The Mother will hug the nurse very tightly. The anesthesiologist will then apply a local numbing agent to the skin, where he will inject the needle. Once the skin is numb, the needle is injected into her lower back, very close to her spine. It is crucial that your partner sits still and hugs the nurse tight for a safe, effective epidural that will work.

Your partner will be offered a doula. A doula stays with your partner while in labor, giving her support and a helping hand. Doulas can be important, especially to women who don't have anyone there with them. Yes, that actually happens and is very sad. Doulas are excellent support for women alone during labor or that need additional help. They are also great for every woman because they can advocate for them and offer unbiased opinions when the family attempts to force her to do what they want. They are also good company.

Unless COVID restrictions are still in order, three people will be allowed in the delivery room to see the child be born. Two of the people in the room will both have to hold one of your partner's legs when she is ready to push.

It is important that you do not drop her leg or allow her to drop them. A woman I know had an epidural, but it only worked on one side of her body. She was in excruciating pain during delivery and very exhausted. Her labor was also a very long one.

When it was finally time to push, she felt defeated after the first few pushes and tried to drop her legs while pushing the baby out. She didn't know that this could break the little one's neck. Thankfully, the doctor caught her leg as she tried to force it from her child's father's arms. The baby was delivered safely.

BIRTHING ASSISTANCE FOR COMPLICATIONS

Childbirth alone has many risks. However, with so many new medical advancements today, doctors have the means to ensure most babies are delivered safely. Sometimes natural childbirths need a little assistance for many reasons.

To assist natural childbirths, doctors use a variety of methods. Forceps delivery is one method of helping natural childbirth. Forceps delivery assistance involves using curved instruments to facilitate the infant's progress in the birth canal. This assistance method is usually used when the Mother is too exhausted to finish delivery herself.

Vacuum extraction is another method used for assistance in natural childbirth. In a vacuum extraction,

a soft cup is placed on the infant's head, and with a hand pump, the doctor will create a suction that will facilitate the baby's delivery. This assisted birth option has a much lower risk for fetal distress than a c-section and has a very low risk of injury to the newborn.

Some women may have the most normal low-risk pregnancy for nine months only to have significant complications at delivery time. A friend of mine has a grandmother who was one of these women who had a normal pregnancy. However, the worst and unexpected happened when she went into labor and delivered her baby. The baby's cord got wrapped around the baby girl's neck. My friend's grandmother lost her baby girl when she delivered her due to this, despite having a normal and healthy pregnancy. This complication doesn't happen as much now as in the past, but it still happens. You should be aware of complications that arise during delivery.

The umbilical cord wrapping around the baby's neck and compression of the umbilical cord by the baby's head in the birthing canal are two of the most significant and dangerous complications at delivery. If doctors notice this early enough, they will perform emergency C-sections; and, in most cases, save the baby.

The baby trying to come out shoulder first, known as shoulder dystocia, is another complication that can arise during pregnancy. Thankfully, this pregnancy complication is not life-threatening. Shoulder Dystocia happens when the baby's anterior shoulder gets hung up above the Mother's pubic bone. When this happens, the baby may suffer from a clavicle fracture. The Mother may get vaginal tears, or her uterus may rupture. The injuries that can occur from this make this an emergency. Thankfully, death from this complication is very rare.

Premature labor is another complication many women have to deal with during pregnancy. Sometimes your partner's healthcare provider can stop premature labor. However, there are many times that they cannot. There have been women that have delivered babies in their second trimester. A long time ago, babies delivered this early had a low chance of survival. Advances in modern healthcare have improved these odds, and now babies born this early have a pretty good chance at survival but a longer hospital stay.

8

FROM THIRD BASE TO
HOME RUN

Your partner did a fantastic job delivering your new teammate. You showed incredible support too, Dad. The two of you joined the game and showed them who the real champions were. You won the MVP trophy with all the help and support you have given. You got the first game in the bag, but now you have many more to go.

Before they let your two teammates run to home plate, they will have to stay in the hospital for a couple of days. On average, most women spend two days in the hospital reviving from the big game. If your partner is getting her tubes tied, she may have to stay a few extra days.

There are a few things you should know about this hospital stay. First of all, you should stay with your partner in the hospital. If you can't, you should at least be there as much as possible. She just pushed life out of her body, and she is hurting. She may need something and feel more comfortable asking you than the nurses. She will also have to make some decisions that you should be a part of.

Most importantly, you must be around to sign the birth certificate. Not only will the child wonder why you didn't later in life if you don't sign it, but signing the birth certificate can help you with visitation rights later if your relationship doesn't work out. After all, the child is yours too and is now your responsibility. Your partner delivered the baby, but it is as much yours as it is hers.

In the hospital, your partner can let the child sleep in the room with her or in the nursery. The benefit of allowing the child to stay in the room with your partner is that it gives the child time to bond with you both immediately. However, Mom just went through something that we men will never be able to understand fully. She needs rest. If I were you, I would let the baby sleep in the nursery because when you get home, the fun begins. I don't mean literal fun, either.

You would need to decide whether or not your child should undergo Circumcision if you had a boy. The choice of Circumcision can be important if you are a religious person. I would have my son undergo Circumcision because uncircumcised baby boys can get many different infections. The choice, though, is up to you and your partner to make together.

The nurses will ask if you have a pediatrician picked for your little one. If you still need to choose one, they will give you a list to choose from when you are ready. Sometimes the pediatrician you have chosen will visit the baby in the hospital. Other times, they like to see the baby the first week they are home from the hospital.

In the hospital, a photographer will come and take photos of your family's new addition and give you a photo order form. You should remember to pack picture outfits for your little superstar. They will also ask you if it is okay to place your baby's photo and name on the hospital website, and sometimes the newspapers print the names of newborn babies.

The nurses will review important baby care information you want to hear. They will teach you the proper way to feed and burp your baby. They will make sure you know how to change the baby's diaper and clothes.

They are so sweet. They will even show you the proper way to swaddle the baby.

While in the hospital, if the nurses notice any problems with the baby taking the formula or breast milk, they will try to sort it out before you leave the hospital. Sometimes it is found that regular formula hurts the baby's belly. If so, they will switch the baby's formula to soy formula because it's easier on their stomach.

The baby's blood will be drawn, and some states will test for illegal drugs to see if the Mother was doing drugs while pregnant. If drugs are found in your little one's system, looking over your state laws is a good idea. Your partner should never do drugs while pregnant because it harms her and your child.

Your baby will also receive an APGAR score when they are born. The APGAR score is a test that measures the baby's heart rate, breathing, muscle tone, reflex response, and your baby's color. This test helps doctors estimate your baby's general condition at birth.

Most newborns score higher than seven on the APGAR test. Newborns that score between five and seven may have experienced problems during birthing that caused lowered oxygen in their blood. Newborns that score less than five are usually premature babies or babies that require an emergency c-section to be delivered.

Scores lower than five may indicate problems with the baby's heart as well as issues with the respiratory system.

The doctors and nurses will also be tending to the Mother right after delivery to ensure that she is okay too. After delivering your superstar, they will hand you or your partner the baby. Most of the time, your partner is the first to hold the baby after the doctor. Right now, you and your partner will only touch the baby briefly. All of your family's fans, who have been cheering you on and anticipating the little one's arrival in the waiting room, will be allowed back, two or three at a time.

After everyone gets to say hi to your little bright-eyed baby, the nurses will shoo them away and get momma settled into a regular hospital room. At this time, your main priority should be getting your partner whatever she wants to eat.

After birth, your partner will be bleeding heavily for about a month. The nurse will teach your partner how to care for herself during this time. She does not need you to do anything to help her with this unless she asks.

Some women tear their skin near the vagina or inside the vagina when delivering the baby and need stitches. If this happens, the doctor puts the stitches in at the time of delivery, and the nurse will teach her how to care for the stitches. She also may get hemorrhoids when pushing during delivery. The hospital will give her witch hazel wipes to soothe everything going on and a nice little squirt bottle that she can fill with soapy water to assist her.

Blood will be drawn from your partner to ensure she is still in good health after giving birth and to ensure she does not need a blood transfusion due to low iron levels or blood loss. They will also check her woman parts a few times before leaving if she re-tore or has complications.

If she decides she wants her tubes tied, they will perform the surgery while she is there. This procedure will add a day or two to her stay. Most women will not be allowed to have their tubes tied if this is their first child. Doctors believe most women will regret it later if they have their tubes tied after giving birth to only one child.

FIRST MONTH HOME

You didn't think I would leave you hanging about what to do when you finally got your baby home, did you? Don't worry; I've got you covered. I will give you a few pointers on making sure things are going right with your baby, partner, and yourself. I will tell you all the important stuff you should know and look forward to as you journey through this first month with your new little bundle of joy. Dad, you have to remember to look after yourself too. You have been so supportive and helpful during this pregnancy, and you must remember to look after yourself too.

Baby's First Month Home

During your baby's first month at home, they will continue to grow into themselves. The baby's muscles will relax after being cramped and balled up in your partner's uterus. You may notice that your baby's sex organs are slightly swollen, but that is okay. This swelling is due to the hormones still running wild through their body from being in utero and will settle down very soon. Many babies lose a little bit of weight after coming home. If yours is one of those many babies, try not to worry. I assure you that everything is okay.

I know many of you want to know about your baby's sleep and how much they do so. From both your and your partner's lack of sleep, you may believe that babies never get any shut-eye or allow you to. You would be shocked to know that, even though it may seem like your child never sleeps because you and your partner are so tired, they sleep a lot. The average baby gets around 16.5 hours of sleep a day. That means they sleep over half the day.

You're probably shaking your head in disbelief right now. Your baby sleeps a lot, just not when you sleep. That is why you are so tired. You and your partner must try to rest when the baby is resting. Many parents try to schedule a sleep schedule around their baby's sleeping times.

I know you are tired, Dad, but Mom has been through a lot. She is sore and hurting right now and needs time to recover. At this stage, is when she needs your support the most. If you see your partner finally getting some shut-eye and you hear the baby cry, go ahead and tend to the baby without waking her up.

Babies eat a lot. During the first month at home, they will eat an average of 12 times every 24 hours (Felton, 2021). When you feed the baby, it's important to let the bubbles in the bottle settle before giving the baby the bottle. If they swallow too much air, their stomachs will feel gassy, and they will let you know about it by screaming at the top of their lungs. It's a great idea to have the gas drops nearby.

While feeding the baby, you should remove the bottle from their mouth and burp them at least twice. Doing this action will also help them with gas issues. Some people prefer to burp the baby by laying it on their shoulders and patting their backs. Others sit the baby upright on their knees, then hold the baby's face with their thumb on one side of the baby's cheek and the rest of their fingers on the other. Once the baby is in the correct position, they pat the baby's back with their free hand—this way, I have found to work best when burping the baby.

Babies tend to scratch their faces a lot. It's important to have a lot of baby gloves. If you do not, it will look like your little superstar got in a fight with Freddy Krueger and lost. The scratches will not feel very good to your baby either and will cause them to cry more.

By the time your baby is one-month-old, they should be able to do the following:

- Lift head briefly during supervised tummy time.
- Focus on faces that they see.
- Bring their hands to their face.
- Make noises other than crying.
- Smile in response to smiles.
- Eat at least every 3-4 hours.
- Respond to sound.
- Have a tight grasp.
- Have a sense of smell.

- Developed their reflexes

Your Partner's First Month Home

Your partner, whether she had a c-section or natural birth, will be recovering this first month. If she had a c-section, it would take her longer to heal, and she will need extra help. The same is true for women who had their tubes tied before leaving the hospital. Mothers who had an excellent natural birth with no complications will also need time for recovery.

Your partner will be bleeding for a week or two. Her bleeding will be heavier than usual when she is on her period. A lot of things are going on down under for your partner, most of which can feel pretty uncomfortable. Not only will she be bleeding, but she may also have hemorrhoids from pushing during delivery and stitches from her perineum tearing during delivery.

You and your partner should not have sex for six weeks after delivery so that her vagina can heal. However, many women do not follow this no-sex rule. They still have sex and have more children born in the same year. Right after pregnancy, you are very, if not the most, fertile.

None of this is fun for a woman, and, on top of a crying newborn and getting no sleep; mom may be a little bit snappy and moody. Try to be patient with her. Her hormones are not yet back to normal. Also, try to ensure that mom gets a lot of rest during this time.

Sometimes, women can get the baby blues the first couple weeks after delivery. These "baby blues" are typical and will disappear once her hormones are balanced. However, sometimes the baby blues do not go away and worsen. If her symptoms worsen, your partner may need to speak to her healthcare provider about postpartum depression, which can become very dangerous and usually occurs 1-3 weeks after pregnancy.

It would be best to watch your partner to ensure she is not showing signs of postpartum depression, as it is associated with causing new mothers to harm them-selves and their babies. There have been new mothers who have killed their babies due to postpartum depres-sion. This disorder can cause the Mother to have psychosis, along with visual and auditory hallucinations.

Some symptoms caused by postpartum depression are:

- Excessive weeping
- Anxiety
- Sleep disturbances
- Anger

- Feeling disconnected from the baby
- Sadness
- Irritability
- Feeling overwhelmed
- Psychosis
- Hallucinations
- Feeling empty, emotionless, and sad
- No interest in the baby
- Feel that they are not a good mother
- Thoughts of hurting herself or the baby

There are no confirmed causes of postpartum depression. Doctors and scientists do believe that postpartum depression could be related to the following (Yim et al., 2015):

- Decrease in hormones
- History of mood disorder
- Sleep disturbances
- Lack of support from family
- The child's father is absent
- Recent divorce
- Loss of a loved one
- Financial stress
- History of depression

You must keep an eye out for signs of postpartum depression in your partner. The earlier postpartum depression is found, the easier it is to get your partner back to normal and feel like herself again. Remember to be supportive and understanding of your partner.

The Mother of your child will have follow-up visits with her doctor to make sure she is healing okay. There is usually nothing to worry about. Most women heal perfectly fine from pregnancy. Others, though, may develop other health problems. Pregnancy takes a lot out of you.

Mom may be protective over the baby, which is entirely normal. It is only natural. You should encourage her to let others help her by watching after the baby, even if it is just for a few hours, so that she can have time to herself and rest. Some moms are just super moms and think they can do it all. Don't expect your partner to be like other moms because every mom is different.

Sometimes the dad is overprotective and doesn't want anyone else to watch the baby. Dad, you need to understand at this time that your partner needs rest. Never leave your child with just anyone, but allow close family and friends you trust to help out with the baby when they offer–even if you and your partner want alone time together. Your partner's hormones are going crazy right now, and receiving help will relieve her.

Dad's First Month Home

Dad, your first month home with the baby is critical. You are the caregiver right now. You have to keep an eye out for Mom and the baby. Being the backbone at this time can get exhausting.

You run to a crying baby and then a crying mother. The baby and Mother are both going through hormone changes. The Mother is healing, and the baby is not sleeping when you and the mom are sleeping. On top of all this, you are probably holding down a job.

You must remember that you can only work, take care of your baby, or help your partner out if you remember to care for yourself. You get overwhelmed and exhausted just as your partner does. You're also losing sleep and having to hold down a job still.

Many men feel like it is selfish at this time to feel exhausted and need some rest. If you feel like this, you shouldn't. It is okay for you to ask for help and time to rest. Discuss your feelings with your partner like you expect her to tell you how she feels and what she needs. She will understand, especially if you have understood her. You two are a team.

To care for yourself, make sure you are getting some rest and sleep. Going for walks is something you can do with your partner and your baby as a family. It is good to get fresh air. Staring at walls all day is unsuitable for you or your partner. Break in your baby's new stroller and walk around the block as a family.

Make sure you are eating well. Have dinner as a family now if you didn't before. It may be easier for you and your partner to have dinner while the baby is asleep. That will also give you two some time together because, as you may be finding out, it's been hard to have alone time with your partner.

Most of all, know that you are doing your best, which has been amazing. You are supportive, caring, loving, understanding, and so much more. You are the definition of a real man and a loving father. All dads reading this, stop right now and pat yourself on the back because you're *the man*!

POSTPARTUM EMOTION SURVIVAL

After coming home with the baby, my wife had a rather hard time with postpartum depression, which, I learned personally, can cause anger and irritability to its fullest. One day, my wife was more upset than usual and started lashing out at me for no reason. Even if I breathed too loud, she would snap at me and tell me to shut up before I woke up the baby.

I would have snapped right back at her in the past because her attitude was uncalled for. I had grown a lot during this pregnancy, though, and learned that many changes were happening inside of my wife both during and after pregnancy. Instead of being angry with her, I felt terrible and understood her. I didn't want her to be so upset during what was supposed to be such a happy time in our lives.

I took a deep breath and asked her if we could discuss what was bothering her so I would know how to help her. As soon as I asked her this, she started crying. She was crying so hard that she could hardly catch her breath. Sliding closer to her on the sofa, I held her and let her cry it out. When my wife was able to talk, she told me all her worries, fears, and how exhausted she had been, and, on top of all that, she told me she felt like a terrible mom for feeling the way she did.

The whole time she talked, I listened attentively and took in what she was saying. I wanted my wife to be happy again. I also wanted her to enjoy being a new mother.

I started taking more responsibility for our baby and doing more household chores. Doing this took a heavy load off my partner's shoulders and gave her peace of mind. She knew then that I cared because I listened to her first, for starters, and then I went a step further. I

actually tried to do something about the way she was feeling. Me doing so let her know I had her back.

If the baby were fussy, I would take the baby from her arms and sit on our porch with him. Doing this gave my little one some fresh air and my wife time to rest.

I kept being patient with her and understanding. Communicating openly and not getting defensive helped a lot. She became less overwhelmed and started apologizing to me when she was snappy. After seeing that, I actually listened to her and tried to help with what was stressing her. She even thanked me many times for doing the smallest of things. Our home slowly adjusted, and we returned to our regular happy routine in no time.

9

ROOKIE DAD'S CHEAT SHEETS

Your superstar is here, and you have learned so much in such a short amount of time. You have learned of every step regarding the development of your little bundle of joy, your partner's symptoms, and each step of her journey. Most importantly, you have survived the big game day: your child's birth. What are you supposed to do now that the baby is here?

Well, many men wonder about this question, so I'm not going to leave you hanging. In this chapter, I will answer new dads' most common questions about this early stage of fatherhood and their partner's postpartum.

This guide will be like your sidekick. You won't have to spend your time scrolling through Google and still not finding the answer to the question on your mind. Nope, all you will need is to open up the book to this chapter. From the basics to the unexpected, these rookie dad cheat sheets got you covered, buddy.

RANDOM NEW DAD QUESTIONS

What should I do if the baby won't stop whining?

Sometimes babies get sick, and sometimes they get hurt. However, they can't tell us what is wrong. There are steps we all should take to figure out what is wrong. First things first, check your baby's diaper to see if it needs to be changed. If so, change it. If the diaper doesn't need to be changed, make funny faces or talk to your baby to see if they want your attention. If they are still not happy, it may be time to eat. Make a bottle and feed the baby. Remember to burp the baby every now and then while feeding. Burping the baby reduces gas pain. If the baby has just finished eating and is still very fussy, then grab the gas drops. Gas drops help reduce the bubbles in their tummy. Not burping your child during feeding can contribute to gas. Bottles that are on the cheap side also can give babies gas. If the baby is fussy after gas drops, it's best to call the doctor.

How can I be more involved during breastfeeding sessions?

If your wife is breastfeeding, you can always help by preparing whatever she needs. Hand her the baby and then anything else she needs, like a cover if she uses one. Some women don't want you all up on them when they are breastfeeding. Many women want privacy during breastfeeding. If your partner wants privacy during breastfeeding, you should stay nearby in case she needs you for something. Stay in ear range, so you can hear her if she calls you for assistance.

How should I hold and carry my baby securely?

Always hold the baby's head when you have them. They cannot yet hold their own heads up. Making sure you support the baby's head and neck is the biggest rule when holding a baby.

How do I change a girl's diaper?

This is an excellent and important question. When changing a baby girl's diaper, you never wipe her back to front. Doing so could give her a UTI or yeast infection if poop gets in her female parts. You always wipe a baby girl front to back.

How do I prevent diaper rash, and what should I do if my baby gets one?

Always keep the baby's diaper area clean and dry to prevent diaper rash. Use powder so the material of the diaper does not rub your baby's bottom too much. Make sure the diapers you have fit just right for your baby. Hypoallergenic diapers are great for babies, especially girls. Diaper rash happens to every baby superstar, though. If yours gets a diaper rash, buy diaper rash cream and keep the area dry. The powder will also soothe the diaper rash. Some diaper rashes are caused by an allergic reaction to the brand of diapers you use. Try changing brands and see if that helps. If diapers are a little too expensive for you, there is always the option of reusable cloth diapers. Cloth diapers save you money and make your baby's bottom happy. However, they aren't the best route to go when you are going to be away from home for a little while.

How do I make a bottle and feed my baby?

All babies are different when it comes to eating. Some are bottle-fed, while others are breastfed. There are also a ton of different types of formulas. Have your partner write down how many scoops of the formula goes into one bottle and how much water. Just a word of advice, putting water in bottles to have them ready to go helps a lot for dads and middle-of-the-night feedings. It also helps when the baby is screaming, and you already have the water in the bottle.

After you put the formula into the bottle of water, you must shake the bottle very well. Make sure the bottle has no lumps of formula in it. You also should wait to feed the baby until all the bubbles are out of the bottle. Doing this makes sure the baby does not swallow air bubbles. If they swallow air bubbles, it could give them gas.

While feeding, hold your baby so that their head is up a little. You should burp your child at least twice during the feeding and once after.

If your wife has chosen to breastfeed, she should pump breast milk for you to give your little one when she is not around. You would feed a breastfed baby the same way as a bottle-fed baby, except you can not microwave the breast milk if your wife freezes it for later use. You must either let it thaw and use it immediately or place it in boiling water to warm up.

How do I make sure I hook the car seat correctly?

Car seats are crucial, and installing them can be highly tricky, no matter which one you get. A car seat can save your child's life, though. That being said, if you do not know what you're doing and are not confident about it being correct in the end, let someone else do it who knows how. To ensure that you have it installed in the car correctly, police stations and fire departments in the U.S. allow you to bring the car seat to them, and they will hook the seat correctly. Doing it this way is best so your little one stays safe while in the car.

How can I help my baby sleep better?

You can do many things to help your child sleep better. The company Johnson & Johnson makes a nighttime body wash and bubble bath. It smells so good and relaxing. The relaxing smell helps your baby relax and sleep, well, like a baby.

It's always good to give your baby a bath right before bed. Lather them down with the matching bedtime lotion when you get them out of the water. Ensuring the baby's belly is good and full before the bath will also help them sleep.

Make sure you invest in a glider or rocker to rock the baby. Some babies do not sleep well. A friend of mine has a child who had night terrors after falling asleep. Night terrors are different from nightmares; if your child has them, the first episode will scare you. Night terrors happen when something in the child's natural sleep cycle is off.

Let me remind you that it is not a bad dream. The difference between the two is when a child has a night terror; they scream bloody murder with their eyes open. Having open eyes leads the parent to believe that their child is awake. However, even though they look awake, they are not. It is important not to wake them because it could scare them even more than it scares you.

Children sometimes wet themselves and shake during night terrors when they get older. These actions make a parent believe the child may have had a seizure. However, they didn't have a seizure. What helped my friend, surprisingly, was running the vacuum. A vacuum sounds very much like the inside of the womb they came out of, so it is soothing to them. Talk to your doctor if your child has been waking up like this in the middle of the night.

Ask your doctor if melatonin is okay to give your child. Melatonin has become very popular with many mothers. It is a vitamin that helps you sleep better and regulates your sleep cycles. Always ask your child's doctor before giving your child any new medicines and vitamins.

What things can I do to bond with my baby?

You can bond with your baby in countless ways. You can hold and talk to them. Babies love to have conversations even though you can't make out their words yet.

146 | ALEX CIRILLO

Singing to babies is another way you can bond with them. My best advice about bonding with babies is just to be a dad. Play with them and spend time with them; when you do, make sure you are actually paying attention to them. Little babies like funny things. The sillier you are, the better you will bond. The sweeter you are, the more you will connect with the baby. Make sure to conversate with them a lot as well. When you have conversations with your baby, they get used to talking to you. They will feel more comfortable coming to you in the future when something is wrong.

Is it selfish if I feel exhausted too?

It is not selfish for you to feel tired and exhausted at all. You have to work and then come home to make the mom and baby happy. You get stressed and worried just as much as mothers do. You must let your partner know if you are exhausted. The two of you could work out a schedule so that each of you gets the time you both need and deserve.

Do I really need to suck my baby's nose out with the nose sucker?

Yes! If your little one's nose is all stuffy, go ahead and suck those boogers out of their nose. They will scream and act like it is killing them, but they are fine. Believe me; my child was the worst when it came to nose-sucking. However, once you finally suck that baby's nose and they see that they can breathe, they will stop crying. Doing this will also allow them to get a better night's sleep since they can breathe better.

How soon can I bathe my newborn?

You should wait until the umbilical stump falls off before giving a new baby a full bath. Before then, you can wash them down with warm, soapy water. If you absolutely need to give them a bath, in the instance of a diaper explosion, be extra cautious of their umbilical cord. It is always best to follow our healthcare providers' recommendations about when to bathe your little superstar. Also, go by their recommendations about umbilical cord care.

WHEN TO CALL THE DOCTOR

Many times it's hard for a first-time mother to know when to call the doctor. If the Mother doesn't know when to call, how are we fathers supposed to know? Below I have composed a list of issues that require you to contact the coach of this pregnancy for the next play:

Your Partner Is Bleeding Out of Their "End Zone"

It is usual for some women to experience light spotting during vaginal exams and after intercourse. It is so common that women hardly ever know when to worry and when not to. Blood from spotting may range from pinkish to brown. So how is anyone supposed to know when to worry about bleeding? If your partner is experiencing period-like cramping, bleeding, abdominal pain, and tightness, then it is time to go to the emergency room for an assessment. Try to stay calm. There may be nothing wrong, but a physician should still evaluate her.

The Baby Isn't Moving

Nothing is scarier for new mothers than when the baby in her stomach has stopped moving, or movement has decreased. Experiencing this can cause any mother to be terrified and stressed. The baby isn't only important to the Mother but also to the dad as well.

When your baby has stopped moving in your partner's belly, have her lay on her right side. While she is lying on her side, ask her to be as still as possible, and the two of you should take kick counts. Kick counts are when you count how many times your baby moves. Count every kick, jab, scratch, roll, and summersault the baby makes. Count all flutters too.

If the baby is still stubborn, drink some orange juice and try again in a few minutes. A little sugar always helps. If the baby does not make at least ten movements in two hours, skip the call to the doctor and go straight to the emergency room. Try not to worry; everything may be okay. Your baby may be a bit lazy today, but it's always better to be safe than sorry.

Upper Right-Sided Abdominal Pain

This advice comes from the experience of a close friend of mine. If your partner experiences upper right-sided abdominal pain that almost brings her to her knees, she may have gallstones. Many women get gallstones when they become pregnant. The pain women experience with gallstones starts in the upper right side of the abdomen, under the right breast, and then radiates to the upper right side of the back, behind the scapula.

This severe pain feels like a very tight, squeezing, crampy pain. This pain will bring you to your knees in seconds. The main sign that the culprit might be gallstones is that the pain will subside in about 3-30 minutes, depending on the severity. After the pain goes away, a dull, achy, or exhausting pain may linger for a few hours. You can also feel these attacks coming on before they happen.

Again, a friend of mine experienced gallstones during pregnancy. Her experience goes to show why good care during pregnancy is crucial. When she became pregnant with her first child, she began to experience pain from gallstones. At first, her pain was mild and not very long-lasting. Her first episode lasted about four minutes. With each episode, the pain got worse and longer.

She spoke with her family and doctor. Most of her family told her to stop complaining about the same pain every pregnant woman in history has dealt with. Her doctor said it was probably reflux; she was given an ultrasound shortly after. After the ultrasound, the doctor's nurse called her and told her everything was normal. She went through her whole pregnancy experiencing these episodes.

She got to the point where she would feel them coming on and excuse herself from whatever room she was in to go into her bedroom, where she would lie down. After lying down, the pain would hit very fast and hard. She would roll back and forth, crying in pain. This pain continued after she gave birth to her son. One night, she excused herself from the room and never came back.

The child's father went to check on her, and she was still crying after 45 minutes and could not move to get anyone. He ran to get her Mother, and he carried her to the car. Her mom started heading toward the ER, but after getting halfway there, the pain subsided. The ER did an ultrasound as soon as they arrived. Her gallbladder was packed so full of large gallstones that they had already loaded into the biliary ducts. There were a few in her pancreas as well. The doctor thought he would have to remove her gallbladder, biliary duct, and pancreas, but he was able to save half the biliary duct and her pancreas. This complication could have all been avoided if the first ultrasound or doctor's nurse had been more thorough.

Colds and Illness

Some over-the-counter medications are not okay to take during pregnancy. It is best to call your doctor if your partner isn't feeling well so that she gets the proper care.

Contractions

Contractions can be tricky. Before your partner begins to have real contractions, she will have Braxton Hicks contractions. These are also known as practice contractions. You do not need to call the doctor for these. However, if your partner has lost her plug and is having contractions that get closer in timing and stronger each time, contact your doctor. If her water has broken, she will start having contractions almost immediately, call the doctor and let them know you are on your way to the hospital.

Lower Abdomen Pain or Cramping

If your partner is experiencing new or worsening cramps, it is always a good idea to mention it to their doctor. If the cramps are followed by blood, one of you should call their OB-GYN right away.

Your Partner's Water May Have Broken

Did a whole lot of liquid fall out of your partner? If so, her water has broken. It is time for the baby to come. Call your doctor immediately and tell them you are on your way to the hospital. If you do not have a vehicle, call the ambulance pronto.

If you have other home birthing options planned, get everything in order. Your baby is coming, and they come fast when you are not in the hospital to deliver. This is the moment you both have been waiting so long for.

STDs

If you or your partner has gotten an STD, you both should see your doctor immediately. STDs can be passed from the Mother to the child during birth. Some STDs can not be cured, such as AIDs and HIV. It is imperative to practice safe sex if you are sleeping with other people. No baby deserves to have STDs at birth.

Falls

Many pregnant women are rather clumsy due to the new body weight that puts them off balance. Remember to remind your partner to hold on to handrails when walking stairs and to wear flat shoes. Heels cause many pregnant women's falls. If your partner does fall down, she should see a doctor whether she feels hurt or not.

HOSPITAL BAG CHECKLIST

Okay, Dad, when the big moment comes, and your partner's water breaks, all she will think about is the pain of the contractions. She will not think about a hospital bag or care about what is in it. Your partner will probably just tell you to grab it. Now, when you get to the hospital and ease her pain, she will want to know if you got the hospital bag and, by God, everything she wants better be in it.

For this reason, it is good to have the bag packed early into the third trimester. Now, we men don't know everything that should go into a hospital bag. That is why I am going to help you out. Below I have included a little cheat sheet and checklist for you to go by when packing the labor and delivery hospital bag.

Things that you should pack in the bag are:

- Health insurance card
- Pre-registration forms from the hospital
- Breast pads
- Nightgown or sleep clothing for your partner and yourself
- Slippers
- Socks
- Outfits for the baby. And remember one for newborn photos!
- Toiletries
- Sanitary pads
- Hair clip to pull back hair for labor
- Extra washcloths
- Magazines or books to read
- Pregnant women may have mints during labor.
- Lollipops or other hard candies will be the only food she is allowed to put in her mouth, so don't forget them.
- Glasses or contact case
- Baby book, if you have one
- Large envelope or file folder for the documents you bring home from the hospital.
- Going home clothes for mom
- Booties/socks for baby
- Receiving blankets

- Newborn and preemie diapers
- Mittens for Baby
- Wipes
- Dad's change of clothes
- Snacks for dad
- Quarters for a vending machine
- Camera or video camera
- Phone

If you have other children, bring:

- Crayons, markers, and coloring books
- Toys for the waiting room
- Snacks and drinks
- A gift from them for their new baby sibling. *Kids love this.*
- A gift from them to Mom. Kids also love to give their moms a gift at times like this.
- Phone or tablet for them to play and watch on. It might be quite a while until they meet their new baby brother or sister, so it's best to keep them busy.

Don't freak out. I know it may seem like you are moving into the hospital with this very long list. The hospital is not going to keep you forever, so don't worry. However, you will need everything on this list and should also think of anything that this list does not have on it that you may need. If you do forget something, though, don't worry. You can always ask a family member to return to your house for whatever you forgot after your baby's birth.

THINGS NOBODY MENTIONS

1. Your partner's ankles will swell, and her feet will hurt
2. Doctor's appointments will make you miss a lot of work.
3. Family, friends, and strangers will talk about your partner's changing body right in front of her.
4. People will try to argue with you up and down about the gender of your baby based on whether your partner is all-belly, packing on the pounds everywhere, and the baby's heart rate.
5. Your partner's body will seem like it has become public property because everybody will try to rub her stomach once she starts showing.
6. Having sex the day before your due date can help your partner go into labor.
7. Heartburn during pregnancy is no joke. Keep Tums nearby for your partner.

8. Whatever you do, do not decide to taste the liquid coming from your partner's breast. It's not technically breast milk yet and doesn't taste very well. Yes, I know this is a crazy fact, but you will be surprised how many dads do this.

9. Boob pain after birth for non-breastfeeders is awful. Pack plenty of cabbage in the freezer or refrigerator so the cold cabbage can be placed into your partner's bra when the pain is in full force. Cold cabbage does wonders for breast pain during and after pregnancy.

10. A lot of women get really horny during pregnancy.

11. Rolling over in the bed for your partner may now feel like she is trying to make a three-point turn in the car.

12. Your partner may fall asleep at random times during her pregnancy.

13. Never tell a pregnant woman that she is or looks fat.

14. Do not mention all of your partner's stretch marks. She doesn't need you to remind her that she has them.

15. Your partner may knock things over with her belly. Sometimes, this can be a little funny, and it is okay to laugh.

158 | ALEX CIRILLO

16. If your partner feels like something is wrong before or after pregnancy, and the doctor isn't doing anything to help, then you need to help her find a second opinion. We have had our bodies as long as we have been alive, so we know better than any doctor when something is wrong and doesn't feel right.

17. Your partner will now be offered the last bit of food wherever she goes. Yes, pregnancy has some perks.

18. Give your child a meaningful name they will love when they grow up. Don't name your child "Pee Wee" if your last name is "Johnson." Remember, the child will have to answer to their name for the rest of their lives.

19. Remember, no two pregnancies are exactly the same.

20. Your partner's sense of smell will seem so strong during pregnancy that it will seem as though they can even sniff out lies.

21. Give her what she is craving. Sometimes the only excitement a pregnant woman gets is eating.

22. Coca-Cola is great for morning sickness, and Mountain Dew will rid your partner of headaches.

23. Your partner's feet will grow.

24. Pregnancy can make your partner's hair change color and texture.
25. Many women develop new health problems after pregnancy.
26. Take advantage of the time you and your partner have together before the baby arrives.
27. Some men are just as rude as some women can be. They will see a pregnant woman standing and still not offer her their seat.
28. You will be scared in the delivery room. You are about to witness your partner's body do things out of this world.
29. Be supportive of each other and one another's opinions during pregnancy. Both your thoughts and feelings matter when it comes to your child. Hear each other out with an open mind. In families, you have to give and take. You can't always have your way and should make decisions based on what is best for your family, not just for yourself or your partner.
30. It's hard to keep a pregnancy quiet.
31. The best feeling in the world is when your partner feels the baby kick for the first time. That is an amazing feeling that many women can't even describe.
32. There is a possibility that your partner may poop herself while pushing the baby out.

33. Women being told they need a C-section can be pretty emotional, so always be supportive of your partner.
34. Many women are scared as hell to give birth.
35. This is the best rollercoaster ride you will ever experience.

FOODS THAT SHOULD NOT BE EATEN DURING PREGNANCY

Your partner has to take many precautions when you are pregnant. Everything she does can affect your growing baby's health. There are many foods that could harm your baby if eaten. Below you will find a list of foods that shouldn't be eaten during pregnancy:

Do Not Eat This Item During Pregnancy	Why Your Partner Should Not Eat It
Raw meats	Raw meats may be contaminated with coliform bacteria, toxoplasmosis, or salmonella, all of which can infect your little one or, even worse, cause miscarriage.
Cold deli meat and spreads.	You should always heat your deli meat before eating it if you are pregnant. Cold deli meat may be contaminated with Listeria. Listeria can cross the placenta to your baby. This can cause your fetus to develop an infection, blood poisoning, and even cause miscarriage.
Raw seafood	Raw seafood contains many bacterias that are very dangerous to your fetus. You should not eat any raw or uncooked seafood until after you have given birth.
Unpasteurized cheese and milk	Both unpasteurized cheese and milk contain a bacteria called Listeria. Listeria, the same bacteria found in cold deli meat, can cause your little one to develop an infection, blood poisoning, and also cause miscarriage.
Pre-made deli salads	Pre-made deli salads not only have cold deli meat in them, but some also contain unpasteurized cheese as well. They also have unwashed vegetables that may be contaminated with toxoplasmosis. Toxoplasmosis is a parasite that is very dangerous to the fetus.

Well, this will do it for your pregnancy journey. You learned a world of things in just a short amount of time. Everything you have learned will help you prepare for pregnancy, delivery, and fatherhood. Your partner will thank you for taking the time to learn about what she and your child are going through during this process. It really shows her that you are just as serious as she is.

In this chapter, I have given you a whole array of random pregnancy "good-to-know" bits to ensure you are prepared for whatever this new journey throws at you. Always remember that no question is too dumb. Nine times out of ten, it is a question everyone else wants to know but is scared to ask. If you can't find the answer in this book, don't be scared to ask your partner's doctor or child's pediatrician.

In the next chapter, I will leave you with a few final thoughts about what is most important when raising your children. The way you raise your children is very important. You should want your child to be a successful, kind human being.

Give other dads-to-be the confidence they need to be the best source of support for their partner.

You now know all the ins and outs of pregnancy and your first month at home.

Simply by leaving your honest opinion of this book on Amazon, you'll help other dads find the answers to all their burning questions. Your first baby isn't nearly as scary when you know about the physical and mental changes your partner will undergo and the needs of your newborn.

WANT TO HELP OTHERS?

Thank you for your help. You can help other men curb their anxiety, prepare for their baby's arrival, and be a calm and confident source of support for their partner.

Scan this QR code to leave a review!

10

FINAL THOUGHTS

Well, my friends, it has been an honor to guide you through your journey of becoming a new father. I hope that you got the answers you needed from this pregnancy guide for men. I want to leave you with a few final thoughts.

First, I want to inform all new fathers that no father is perfect. You may fail at many things in fatherhood the first time, but that's okay. If you never fail, how will you ever learn? What matters the most is that you are there and trying your best. I am proud of how great you all have done so far.

Remember that fathers are very important to their children. They are just as important as mothers are to their children. Fathers help children learn, grow, and become self-confident and social. They instill morals, values, and principles into their children. When raising your child, raise them to treat others how they expect to be treated. Teach them to show compassion and love to everyone, regardless of age, gender, color, race, or financial status. Teach them there is so much more to life than money and material things.

Teach them to help their neighbor when they can. Make sure they know that not all people have the money to buy nice things so that when they start school, they do not bully underprivileged students. Make sure they respect not only their elders but also their peers.

Don't ever feel bad about disciplining your child. Without disciplined children, we would have a world full of hooligans, which we already have if I do say so myself. It is not too late to change all the evil in the world, but the only way to eliminate some of the evil we see every day is to do a better job parenting our children. Remember, they are the future of the world.

Be there emotionally for your child as they grow older. Many parents never realize it, but they don't show their children much emotion, which results in the child suffering from emotional neglect. This neglect could seriously hold them back as they become adults. We have to pay attention to our children more.

Try to make your family work no matter what. The world is really missing the family structure right now. Even if there is no fixing your family, still do things as a family for your children. Don't let another woman overstep her boundaries with your child's Mother or disrespect her. If you guys don't work out, the same should go for your partner. No other man should be allowed to overstep their boundaries or disrespect you, either. You are a team whether you are together or not, so you should do your best to show good teamwork.

Don't spend fatherhood worrying about money. Spend it teaching your children how to be successful, loving, understanding, and wise adults. Give them great morals, values, and principles to pass down to their own children. Don't dismiss their feelings and emotions. Hear your children out. Just because they are children doesn't mean they don't deserve our respect.

Make sure they get a good education and study hard. Teach them their rights as citizens. Get outside and teach children how to play again and enjoy nature. Build a treehouse or play a game of kickball with them when they get older. Life doesn't always have to be so serious. Relax and have fun.

I think you got this, Dad. You are going to be a fantastic father. Never give up, even on bad days. When you are having a bad day, rest and know that everyone has a bad day now and then, but how you handle those times determines how strong and wise you are. It has been fun. Good luck to every one of you!

REFERENCES

ASPE. (2005, January). *Male Perpetrators of Child Maltreatment: Findings from NCANDS.* Assistant Secretary for Planning and Evaluation. https://aspe.hhs.gov/reports/male-perpetrators-child-maltreatment-findings-ncands-1

Brott, A. A. (2022). *The Importance of dad involvement.* San Diego Family. https://www.sandiegofamily.com/parenting/baby/why-babies-need-dad-involvement

CCBC. (2017). *Water Birth.* Corpus Christi Birth Center. https://www.ccbirthcenter.com/water-birth/#:~:text=The%20theory%20behind%20water%20birth

Coussons-Read, M. E. (2013). *Effects of prenatal stress on pregnancy and human development: mechanisms and pathways.* Obstetric Medicine, 6(2), 52–57. https://doi.org/10.1177/1753495x12473751

Donaldson-Evans, C. (2014a). *Your Pregnancy Week-by-Week.* What to Expect. https://www.whattoexpect.com/pregnancy/week-by-week/#Second-Trimester

Donaldson-Evans, C. (2014b, September 16). *1 and 2 Weeks Pregnant.* What to Expect. https://www.whattoexpect.com/pregnancy/week-by-week/weeks-1-and-2.aspx

Felton, K. (2021, October 25). *Your 1-Month-Old Baby's Biggest Milestones.* What to Expect. https://www.whattoexpect.com/first-year/month-1

Goodreads. (n.d.). *A quote by Osho.* Goodreads. https://www.goodreads.com/quotes/33588-the-moment-a-child-is-born-the-mother-is-also#:~:text=She%20never%20existed%20before

Lack Bradford, E. (2021, March 22). *Pregnancy Symptoms in Men: Couvade Syndrome (Sympathetic Pregnancy).* BabyCenter. https://www.babycenter.com/pregnancy/relationships/strange-but-true-couvade-syndrome-sympathetic-pregnancy_10364940#:~:text=Couvade%20syndrome%20or%20sympathetic%20pregnancy

Lie, R. T., Wilcox, A. J., Taylor, J., Gjessing, H. K., Saugstad, O. D., Aaby-holm, F., & Vindenes, H. (2008). *Maternal Smoking and Oral Clefts.* Epidemiology, 19(4), 606–615. https://doi.org/10.1097/ede. 0b013e3181690731

Rae, M., Cox, C., & Dingel, H. (2022, July 13). *Health costs associated with pregnancy, childbirth, and postpartum care.* Peterson-KFF Health System Tracker. https://www.healthsystemtracker.org/brief/ health-costs-associated-with-pregnancy-childbirth-and-postpar tum-care/

UCSF Health. (2022, December). *Substance Use During Pregnancy.* University of California San Francisco. https://www.ucsfhealth. org/education/substance-use-during-pregnancy#:~:text= Pregnancy-

Wow4u. *57 quotes about helping others.* https://www.wow4u.com/57- quotes-about-helping-others/?utm_content=cmp-true

Yim, I. S., Tanner Stapleton, L. R., Guardino, C. M., Hahn-Holbrook, J., & Dunkel Schetter, C. (2015). *Biological and Psychosocial Predictors of Postpartum Depression: Systematic Review and Call for Integration.* Annual Review of Clinical Psychology, 11(1), 99–137. https://doi. org/10.1146/annurev-clinpsy-101414-020426